The Modern Allegories of William Golding

L. L. Dickson

The Modern Allegories

# of William Golding

University of South Florida Press / Tampa

The University of South Florida Press is a member of University Presses of Florida, the scholarly publishing agency of the State University System of Florida. Books are selected for publication by faculty editorial committees at each of Floridas nine public universities: Florida A&M University (Tallahassee), Florida Atlantic University (Boco Raton), Florida International University (Miami), Florida State University (Tallahassee), University of Central Florida (Orlando), University of Florida (Gainesville), University of North Florida (Jacksonville), University of South Florida (Tampa), University of West Florida (Pensacola).

Orders for books published by all member presses should be addressed to University Presses of Florida, 15 NW 15th St., Gainesville, FL 32603.

Library of Congress Cataloging-in-Publication Data

Dickson, L. L.
   The modern allegories of William Golding / L.L. Dickson.
      p.   cm.
   Includes bibliographical references.
   ISBN 0–8130–0971–5 (alk. paper)
      1. Golding, William, 1911– —Criticism and interpretation.
2. Allegory.   I. Title.
PR6013.035Z615 1990   89–24873
823′ .914–dc20   CIP

for my mother and the memory of my father

Contents

Preface

In the 1960s, when I first started reading literary criticism of William Golding's work, I noticed that one term of evaluation invariably recurred—allegory. Though "parable," "fable," and "myth" were often bandied about, a central idea that emerged in the sixties, and one that has continued with somewhat less force up to the present time, was that each of Golding's novels encapsulated a kind of moral allegory. Yet I was surprised that no critic wanted to discuss in any detail what was meant by "allegory" in the context of the modern novel. I recognized that Golding's novels relied heavily on symbolism and that their creator was inventively forging his own myths in narrative settings that ranged from prehistory to present-day England, but did such patterns of symbolism constitute a type of modern allegory?

Critics either paid brief lip service to the idea that Golding's novels seemed allegorical, and therefore profound, or they chided him for writing with too rigid a thesis. The more I studied Golding's writing and the criticism it evoked, the more I felt a need to clarify in my own mind the extent to which his novels are indeed allegorical. This book is the result of my investigations concerning the structural basis for Golding's art.

In the 1970s, while teaching courses in the recent British

novel, I discovered the works of two theoreticians who had devised systematic and workable approaches to the subject of allegory in the context of modern literature. Edwin Honig, in *Dark Conceit: The Making of Allegory* (1959), analyzes how characterization in the novel can be affected by analogical processes, for the purpose of allegory. Though Honig's study largely concentrates on nineteenth-century American literature, his brief discussion of a few twentieth-century writers suggests the applicability of these critical theories to modern fiction. Angus Fletcher, in *Allegory: The Theory of a Symbolic Mode* (1964), identifies major patterns of allegorical action affecting plot development and investigates the relationship between allegory and imagery. Fletcher, while discussing Spenser, Milton, and Shakespeare at some length, examines some twentieth-century writers and includes short comments on the early novels of William Golding.

These theories of Honig and Fletcher do much to illuminate the workings of allegory in modern literature, and I have drawn on their ideas for the critical basis of my study. My intention, therefore, has been not to devise a new critical theory but to apply concepts of Honig and Fletcher to the novels of William Golding in order to determine whether the term "allegory" is appropriate to these contemporary works.

My purpose in this study, then, is to determine the extent to which each of Golding's novels is a moral allegory—that is, the extent to which the protagonist symbolically reenacts a version of the universal quest to understand the nature of good and evil. I examine all of Golding's novels to 1987.

I am indebted to the late Jack Biles of Georgia State University for his advice when I was first planning this book and to Elinor Welt of Auburn University for her valuable comments on my manuscript. Also John Weigel of Miami (Ohio) University offered considerable help in the early stages of my research. In addition, I am grateful to three of my colleagues at Northern Kentucky University for their aid: Joseph Price clarified some matters pertaining to the language of classical Greek; Robert Collier helped me learn how to write with a word processor; and the chairperson of the Department of Literature and Language, Paul Reichardt, provided valuable release time from my teaching schedule so I could complete this book. A colleague formerly at Northern, Thomas Niemann, supplied useful ideas about allegory in medieval literature and also first called my attention to Angus Fletcher's work.

I am grateful to the following publishers for permission to quote excerpts from Golding's works:

Lord of the Flies, copyright © 1954 by William Gerald Golding, reprinted by permission of Coward, McCann & Geoghegan, Inc., and the Putnam Publishing Group.

The Inheritors, copyright © 1955 by William Golding, reprinted by permission of Harcourt Brace Jovanovich, Inc.

Pincher Martin, copyright © 1957 by William Golding and renewed 1984 by William Gerald Golding, reprinted by permission of Harcourt Brace Jovanovich, Inc.

Free Fall, copyright © 1959 by William Golding, reprinted by permission of Harcourt Brace Jovanovich, Inc.

The Spire, copyright © 1964 by William Golding, reprinted by permission of Harcourt Brace Jovanovich, Inc.

The Pyramid, copyright © 1967 by William Golding, reprinted by permission of Harcourt Brace Jovanovich, Inc.

Darkness Visible, copyright © 1979 by William Golding, reprinted by permission of Farrar, Straus & Giroux, Inc.

Rites of Passage, copyright © 1980 by William Golding, reprinted by permission of Farrar, Straus & Giroux, Inc.

The Paper Men, copyright © 1984 by William Golding, reprinted by permission of Farrar, Straus & Giroux, Inc.

1   Allegory and the Modern Novel

The fiction of William Golding is a unique blending of realism and fable. His novels possess the recognizable qualities of realistic fiction, yet at the same time they incorporate a consistent system of symbolism that allows for an allegorical meaning. Robert Scholes calls this unique mode of writing "modern fabulation," which "tends away from the representation of reality but returns toward actual human life by way of ethically controlled fantasy. Many fabulators are allegorists. But the modern fabulators allegorize in peculiarly modern ways."[1] William Golding is such a fabulator, and his "peculiarly modern ways" are the subject for this study. My purposes are to determine the extent to which Golding's novels are moral allegories, to clarify the way setting, characterization, and narration are affected by the novelist's allegorical purposes, and to consider how imagery relates to allegory and reinforces the large themes of Golding's work. The critical theories of Angus Fletcher and Edwin Honig will prove particularly helpful in clarifying Golding's form of modern allegory.

In a general sense, allegory may be defined as "a form of extended metaphor in which objects, persons, and actions in a narrative, either prose or verse, are equated with meanings that lie outside the narrative itself."[2] One authority adds, "Even when they are most mimetic, allegorical fictions illustrate some further metaphysical, theological, ethical, or social doctrine through the manipulation of images that have stipulated meanings *other than* their meanings as imitations of the actual world."[3] It is the ethical or moral level of meaning that most significantly applies to the modern allegories of William Golding. In each novel, the protagonist's search to understand the nature of evil (often identical with his own nature) is manifested in a symbolic journey, central to the theme. For all their realistic detail, those symbolic landscapes of hell that occur repeatedly in Golding's fiction are reminiscent of the settings for the underworld journeys so prominent in Greek and Roman narrative allegory.

In modern allegory, and particularly in Golding's work, what readers are not likely to find is an infallible relationship by which all events or characters in the novels possess a neat symbolic counterpart. Such a rigid structure of ideas is more properly called "naive allegory," the type of literature that often connotes artificiality, lack of spontaneity, and inflexibility. Unlike naive allegory, modern fabulation allows for greater adaptability. Characters take on a life and fullness of their own, an authenticity as representatives of believable persons engaged in real-life events. In a conversation I had with Golding in 1978, he commented that many traditional allegories lack a "passion" or intensity necessary to good art. In contrast to this idea, the successful *modern* fabulator is able to create a dynamic quality. This vitality is surely the essence of good literature; it embodies the qualities of life, of verisimilitude, of tragedy, of ambiguity, and it transforms mere literary formula into art. In clarifying Golding's system of symbols, I will not call his work unsuccessful, as some critics have done, when ambiguities of character or event preclude neat categorization. It is important to realize that every detail within an allegorical scene need not have added significance. Certainly a chief danger in any study of allegory is overreading.

Golding himself has called *Lord of the Flies* a "fable," and in explaining the suitability of this form to his intention, he observed that "a novelist ought not preach overtly in a fable."[4] Yet in a later interview, he asserted that "the fabulist is always a moralist."[5] In a BBC radio interview with Frank Kermode, the novelist further qualified his own view of fable: "What I would regard as a tremendous compliment to myself would be if someone would substitute the word 'myth' for 'fable' because I think a myth is a much profounder and more significant thing than a fable."[6] He added that fable is too contrived and that myth is more fundamental in its application to the human condition.

In past interviews, Golding has been somewhat wary when discussing the intricacies of allegory. In response to the question of whether Aldous Huxley is more an essayist than a novelist, Golding merely says, "I don't know. Perhaps he is an allegorist, or perhaps he is simply an ideas man. I wouldn't know."[7] In this particular conversation, Golding is more comfortable when categorizing novelists as simply those who are interested in people ("character men") and those who are interested in ideas ("ideas men"), identifying himself with the latter. In my conversations with Golding, I gathered that he believes allegory to be a strict, highly *conscious* ordering of matching relationships, while myth allows for an almost unconscious symbolism, a more desirable, flexible condition for the modern artist, and a more accurate description of what he is doing. Golding favors the term "myth," but as his early novels demonstrate, the vehicle by which he expresses his narrative myths is a type of modern allegory.[8]

The long-standing prejudices against allegory have characterized it as an extreme technique by which details of character or situation mean not only something more than what is directly stated in the text but something totally different from that surface meaning. Such a view has developed from a nineteenth-century distinction between allegory and symbol popularized by Samuel Taylor Coleridge.[9] By identifying symbolism with the organic and allegory with the mechanical, Coleridge stigmatized allegory as artificial and shallow. Coleridge's concept of allegory as a contrivance *imposed* on the subject survives today, though it surely oversimplifies the real function of allegory. Coleridge characterized allegory as merely the mechanical act of translating abstractions into a contrived picture-language; but, on the other hand, the qualities he assigned to symbols—that they were both "general" and "special," "eternal" and "temporal," simultaneously individual and universal—might be just as accurately applied to allegory. Indeed, the medieval concept of allegory allows for this simultaneous "double force." Both the literal and symbolic functions of the narrative occur at the same time, and consequently the medieval notion of allegory provides for the concomitance of the physical with the spiritual, the rational with the mythic.[10]

A recent manifestation of the negative view of allegory occurs in Virginia Tiger's book on Golding. She maintains that allegory must traditionally have four levels of meanings; hence, allegorical literature emerges as an overdidactic, hopelessly contrived, inferior mode of writing.[11] Modern allegorists are simply not compelled to write in such a rigid format. To suggest that there must always be four levels is to impose needless strictures.[12] The use of allegory in no way implies, more than for any other type of literature, a "tendency to reduce life to pattern," as one of Golding's most recent critics, Arnold Johnston, simplistically believes.[13] The novelist has never relied on the kind of predictable didacticism that Johnston implies. Though Golding is clearly interested in "ideas," he is foremost an artist.

It is important to distinguish between naive allegory, which announces that the text "does not mean this, but really means something else," and a more complex view that believes that the text "means this and *also* something else."[14] My study will always refer to this second kind of allegory. Because I will be emphasizing allegory as a structural principle, it is necessary to consider the ways in which the agents, actions, and images of a literary subject are affected by the allegorical mode. For this threefold approach, I will adapt the critical theories of Angus Fletcher, as discussed in his *Allegory: The Theory of a Symbolic Mode*.

Fletcher believes that personified abstractions are the most obvious allegorical agents, but to be truly effective, personified agents, besides representing ideas, must also possess "adequate representational power," a convincing reality of their own. Part of Golding's artistry is that he successfully incorporates larger symbolic meanings into novels that already possess interesting narratives, realistic situations, and believable characters in their own right. Golding's works explore the "double power" associated with medieval allegory and suggest the organic unity that Coleridge assigned only to symbolism.

To clarify the symbolism of Golding's novels, this study will be discussing four techniques that, according to theorist Edwin Honig, contribute to allegorical personification: analogy through the use of names, the correlation of a state of nature with a state of mind, the implied comparison of an action with an extrafictional event, outside novel itself, and the correspondence of a state of mind with an action depicted in the narrative.[15]

According to Honig, analogy through nomenclature establishes an attributive name for a character or place and, "as it constantly designates an event, person, idea, or quality existing outside the story, builds up a sense of like identity in the fiction" (p. 118). Naming characters after vices or virtues is the most obvious manifestation of this process; however, nineteenth-century authors-turned-social-critics like Dickens (or Poe in his short satirical pieces), or symbolists like Hawthorne and Melville, or certainly modern novelists like Thomas Mann, James Joyce, Iris Murdoch, John Updike, to name only a few, have continued to use names to suggest an extrafictional frame of reference. I do not mean to imply that such practices inevitably lead to dull stereotyping, where the agent has no existence of its own. On the contrary, modern fictional characters can, and should, possess particularized human qualities in their own right; the names the author assigns to his characters "suggest both their uniqueness and their universality" (p. 118) at the same time.

If we use Franz Kafka's *The Metamorphosis* as a representative example of modern allegory, we discover analogy through nomenclature upon consideration of the additional meanings contained in the protagonist's name, Gregor Samsa. Not only is the name a possible cryptogram for "Kafka," but more significantly it is "a phonetic contraction of the Czech words *sam* ('alone') and *jsem* ('I am')."[16] Also there is the suggestion of "Samson" (literally "the sun's man"), combining the image of the lowly dung beetle with the sacred scarab linked to sun god worship, an ironic "combination of lothesomeness [*sic*] and divinity."[17] The name "Gregory" (literally "watchful" or "awakened") strengthens the symbolism of the story by implying that Gregor's transformation corresponds with his sudden awareness of his own alienation.

The analogy that compares a state of nature with a state of mind involves the process of humanizing nature—"that is, feeling tender toward it by uniting with and gaining control over it. The personification, then, is as much a matter of reading benignity or malignity into, as of reading it from, the evidence of nature" (p. 119). In *The Metamorphosis* the state of the weather parallels Samsa's own mental disposition or spiritual confusion: "The overcast weather—he could hear raindrops hitting against the metal window ledge—completely depressed him." When he hopes to clear his mind and make sense out of his new state of affairs, the weather outside his window symbolizes his own uncertainty: "At such moments [as he searched for rational order in a world of chaos and social disintegration] he fixed his eyes as sharply as possible on the window, but unfortunately there was little confidence and cheer to be gotten from the view of the morning fog."

The correspondence of an action with an extrafictional event enlarges the significance of the literal action by suggesting an analogue that is either appropriate or inappropriate, the latter especially suited to the more sarcastic views of twentieth-century fiction. Such "extrafictional events" emerge when particulars of the narrative suggest a parallel with classical mythology or with the passion and sacrifice of Christ, to cite two common examples. In comparing the idea of Christ on the cross with Dimmesdale's scaffold scene in *The Scarlet Letter* and then with the ordeal of Kafka's caged Hunger Artist, Honig notes that both writers, like most modern allegorists, use the analogue for purposes of irony:

> Neither allegorist intends the analogy to be taken as a literal reconstruction of the episode described in the Gospels. Hawthorne and Kafka adapt the episode in order to fortify carefully developed symbols of their own: Hawthorne, the scarlet letter and the scaffold, which are harmonized allegorically; Kafka, the cage where the Artist undergoes his fast,

and the carnival at which he is ironically exhibited as a martyr. The analogy on the scriptural episode fuses these symbols with a powerful cultural image which the reader cannot help recognizing. The analogy presents a reenactment of Christ's ordeal, but it is not aimed at supplying a doctrinal example, as with Spenser or Dante. Hawthorne and Kafka seem to be saying that in the situations they set forth the Crucifixion can only be shown obliquely, as an irony. (p. 125)

Similarly, Gregor Samsa's transformation represents a *"negative transfiguration,* the inversion of the Transfiguration of Christ, the Passion of an abortive Christ figure."[18] The scene in which Samsa's father throws apples at him becomes an inversion of the Fall motif. The classical theme of metamorphosis, in Golding as well as Kafka, is used in the manner of Ovid: "The dehumanization of the subject represents either a blessing or a punishment ordained by [an omnipotent power], and the particular physical change reflects an appropriate moral judgment."[19] In Golding's work, we encounter the punishment of Christopher Martin's metamorphosis into lobster claws (in *Pincher Martin*), as well as the blessing of Matty's consummate transformation into holy fire (in *Darkness Visible*).

Finally, the manifestation in an action of a state of mind invites a psychological reading of the text, by which we determine the protagonist's mental disposition. Samsa's physical inertia ("No matter how hard he threw himself onto his right side, he always rocked onto his back again. He must have tried it a hundred times") symbolizes his own spiritual and social debilitation. His inability to move is analogous to his mental paralysis that results from an oppressive job (he is without "backbone," a mere "tool of the boss") and a loveless family life.

The purpose in defining and illustrating these four types of analogy is to establish a workable method for analyzing fictional "agents" as they are affected by personifications and analogues conducive to allegory. Not only is this method applicable to Kafka's fiction, but a similar analysis of the primary agents of Golding's allegories is also possible. Clearly the third and fourth

analogical resources pertain to action as much as agent; therefore, it is important to understand the direct relationship between actor and action.

In order for an agent to realize its ideational value, it must
involve itself with "action." As Honig observes, "The transvalua-
tion of fictional agents from relatively static ideational figures at
the start of progressively more active and meaningful roles in the
course of the narrative . . . is effected when [the] ideational roles
are fully tested in the action . . . and finally resolved in the larger
design of the allegory" (p. 138). The two fundamental patterns
by which allegorical action is often resolved are "progress" and
"battle."[20] Progress suggests the motif of the journey—whether
plausible or fantastic, whether actual or symbolic—which involves a constant forward motion, "unremittingly directed toward
a goal."[21]

Normally the journey motif is identical with both the ideas
of quest and pilgrimage, but these two terms have sometimes
been distinguished as an outward journey (the quest) to adventure, to new lands, "whether spatial, temporal, or symbolic,"[22] and
an inward journey (pilgrimage) to self-knowledge, understanding, and moral enlightenment. More often than not, however, the
two types function simultaneously, and the exciting physical
adventures are the means for increased awareness and self-
evaluation. *Huckleberry Finn, Moby Dick,* and *Gulliver's Travels*
all incorporate elements of quest and pilgrimage, though the fulfillment of the pilgrimage is an ironic one for Ahab and Gulliver.
Sammy Mountjoy's pilgrimage in Golding's *Free Fall* also takes
the form of quest, even though Sammy's previous ordeals and
war experiences are recollected only in his mind. Similarly, it is
by dramatically overcoming the spectacular—and physical—
architectural challenges of constructing a four-hundred-foot
tower that Dean Jocelin of *The Spire* moves from an exciting personal adventure to the realm of self-evaluation and moral insight.

The battle motif, the second major pattern of allegorical action, normally involves overt physical confrontation and violence.
Fletcher traces the origin of the battle pattern, as it appears in
Western literature, to Hesiod's account of the gigantomachia (the
battle between the Titans) and then focuses on the psychological

battle allegorized in the *Psychomachia* of Prudentius, the fourth-century Christian poet. C. S. Lewis agrees that "the *bellum intestinum* is the root of all allegory," though he adds that only the crudest allegories represent symbolic conflicts in the guise of actual pitched battles.[23] Lewis criticizes the obviousness of Prudentius's poem and clearly prefers the journey motif as a more suitable vehicle for allegory:

> Seneca, with his imagery of life as a journey, was nearer to the mark than Prudentius. . . . It is not hard to see why this should be so. The journey has its ups and downs, its pleasant resting-places enjoyed for a night and then abandoned, its unexpected meetings, its rumors of dangers ahead, and, above all, the sense of its goal, at first far distant and dimly heard of, but growing nearer at every turn of the road. Now this represents far more truly than any combat in a *champ clos* the perennial strangeness, the adventurousness, and the sinuous forward movement of the inner life.[24]

However, the idea of "battle" can be represented through ideological conflicts and rhetorical combats as well as actual physical confrontations. As Fletcher observes, "Common among the gentler permutations of this imagery of conflict are the 'debate' and the 'dialogue' (of Socrates and Euthyphro, of owl and nightingale, of self and soul), where the war is verbal and more ironical and polite than Prudentius' physical struggle."[25] If one acknowledges debate and dialogue as subtle forms of the battle pattern, it is then possible to identify, with maximum flexibility, elements of allegorical action idiomatic to contemporary fiction. The allegorical process involves what Honig has called a "dialectic transfer," by which agents clarify as well as dramatize their ideational roles through action. In Golding's fiction, both patterns of allegorical action—progress and battle—are evident. The double force of Golding's allegory is particularly effective in his dramatic use of the battle motif, where physical struggles, realistically convincing in their own right, enhance the implied symbolic conflicts.

Just as agency and action require a close interrelationship, so does the imagery of an allegory reinforce the symbolic meaning. The term *image* can be classified in three ways. Imagery can refer to the simple "representation through language of sense experience."[26] The depiction of such sense impressions primarily helps expand description. Inasmuch as all the senses can be involved, imagery is by no means limited to merely visual matters. Second, the image can exist as a figure of speech—a metaphor or simile—where the image also refers to "something else," and it is at this point that image and symbol begin to merge. Indeed, a third category emphasizes the capacity of an image to embody a symbolic vision. The difference between the second and third types, then, is largely determined by recurrence. René Wellek and Austin Warren have explained it as follows: "Is there any important sense in which 'symbol' differs from 'image' and 'metaphor'? Primarily, we think, in the recurrence and persistence of the 'symbol.' An 'image' may be invoked once as a metaphor, but if it persistently recurs, both as presentation and representation, it becomes a symbol, [and] may even become part of a symbolic (or mythic) system."[27] It is in this third context, which acknowledges the power of images to function symbolically, that I will use the term *image*.

When Sammy Mountjoy says in the opening chapter of *Free Fall* that "I am shut in a bone box and trying to fasten myself on the white paper," the image not only adds descriptive power and not only functions as an isolated metaphor; it also contributes to a whole series of images that suggest Sammy's symbolic bondage and loss of freedom. Thematically significant imagery, then, can be considered synonymous with symbolism.

The manner in which allegory affects imagery must be examined if Golding's artistic achievement is to be evaluated properly. Close consideration of Golding's imagery will reveal recurring patterns that reinforce the symbolism in each novel. Most prominent are images identified with darkness, falling, excrement, and animalism. These images function symbolically and are obviously connected with negative views of the human situation. Other image patterns are considerably more subtle. But surely in any estimation of Golding's artistry, the way imagery enhances, and is even determined by, allegory must be considered.

I have rejected here the critical view that categorizes allegory as an over contrived and consequently inferior type of symbolism.[28] I have defined allegory as essentially a form of extended metaphor, a form that includes a systematic arrangement of symbols. I have suggested a close connection between myth and narrative allegory.[29] Golding's novels can be clarified by observing the way his allegorical agents realize their ideational value through action, and by considering the relationship between imagery and allegorical meaning.

Because allegory, even in a "modern" context, is not common to the twentieth-century British novel, Golding has earned the reputation as experimenter, parablist, fabulator.[30] At times his fellow novelists have chided him because of his fondness for the abstract, as does Kingsley Amis in a review of *Pincher Martin*: "I hope Mr. Golding will forgive me if I ask him to turn his gifts of originality, or intransigence, and above all of passion, to the world where we have to live."[31] Others have been more encouraging. Angus Wilson, identifying himself as a "reactionary" novelist who has helped revitalize the contemporary novel form, adds, "Orthodoxy of the social novel, however, would be as deplorable as the orthodoxy of Bloomsbury. I should be happy to see more than Mr. William Golding swimming against the tide with success."[32] In the following chapters I will examine in detail the extraordinary novels that account for this success, in order to demonstrate that Golding's works truly belong among the important symbolical novels of twentieth-century literature.

Lord of the Flies 2

Of Golding's nine novels, *Lord of the Flies* is most clearly an allegory. It has been criticized as both too explicit[1] and too ambiguous.[2] Walter Allen's skepticism is typical: "The difficulty begins when one smells allegory."[3] More accurately, Golding's *Lord of the Flies* combines the best features of realistic and allegorical fiction; the novel allows for "the simultaneous operation of the factual and the fabular."[4]

The tension between realistic novel and allegorical fable is established in the setting for the action in *Lord of the Flies:* the isolated island provides an appropriate stage for the survival story of the deserted boys, but also suggests a universal, timeless backdrop for symbolic action. Golding creates a microcosm, a procedure common "to the great allegorists and satirists," and then "examines the problem of how to maintain moderate liberal values and to pursue distant ends against pressure from extremists and against the lower instincts."[5] The protagonist's ironic "rescue" by a naval officer, who is himself engrossed in the savage business of international warfare, reveals that the chaotic island-world is but a small version of a war-torn adult world. The novel does not imply that children, without the disciplined control of adults, will turn into savages; on the contrary, it dramatizes the real nature of all humans. The nightmare world, which quickly develops on the island, parallels the destruction of the outside world through atomic warfare. The dead parachutist, whom the boys mistake for the Beast, is a symbolic reminder of the human history of self-destruction; the parachutist is literally and figuratively a "fallen man."

At first, the island world is compared to Eden: the boys "accepted the pleasure of morning, the bright sun, the whelming sea and sweet air, as a time when play was good and life so full that hope was not necessary and therefore forgotten."[6] But this setting is simultaneously sinister and hostile. The boys are scratched by thorns and entrapped by creepers. "The ground beneath them was a bank covered with coarse grass, torn everywhere by the upheavals of fallen trees, scattered with decaying coconuts and palm saplings. Behind this was the darkness of the forest proper and the open scar" (p. 6). Eventually the island becomes a burning hell: "Smoke was seeping through the branches in white and yellow wisps, the patch of blue sky overhead turned to the color of a storm cloud, and then the smoke bellowed around him" [Ralph, the protagonist] (p. 233). The island is a microcosm from the adult world; indeed, "you realize after a time that the book is nothing less than a history of mankind itself."[7]

THE PERSONIFIED agents in *Lord of the Flies* are developed in all the four ways discussed in the first chapter. First, the analogy through nomenclature is the most obvious method by which the characters take on additional dimensions. Golding's novel represents an ironic treatment of R. M. Ballantyne's *The Coral Island,* a children's classic that presents the romantic adventures of a group of English schoolboys marooned on an Edenlike South Sea island. By mustering their wits and their British courage, the boys defeat the evil forces on the island: pirates and native savages. Not only is Golding's island literally a coral island (p. 12) where the boys "dream pleasantly" and romantically, but there are specific references to Ballantyne: "'It's like in a book.' At once there was a clamor. 'Treasure Island—' 'Swallows and Amazons—' 'Coral Island—'" (p. 37). At the conclusion of the novel, the dull-witted naval officer who comes to Ralph's rescue makes an explicit comparison: "Jolly good show. Like the Coral Island" (p. 242). Golding uses the same names for his main characters as Ballantyne did. Ralph, Jack, and Peterkin Gay of *The Coral Island* become Golding's Ralph, Jack, and Simon ("Simon called Peter, you see. It was worked out very carefully in every possible way, this novel"[8]). Golding's characters, however, represent ironic versions of the earlier literary work, and their very names, inviting comparison to Ballantyne, add ironic impact to the characterization.

The change of Peterkin's name to Simon better supports that character's function as a "saint" figure in Golding's novel. Obviously Piggy's name contributes to the symbolism: Piggy will become identified with a hunted pig, and eventually will be killed too, as the boys' savage hunt turns to human rather than animal victims. When Piggy falls to his death, his arms and legs twitch "like a pig's after it has been killed" (p. 217). Jack's name is a variant of John, the disciple of Christ, and indeed Jack is an ironic distortion of the religious connotations of his name, in the same manner as is Christopher Martin, the egocentric protagonist of Golding's third novel.

Second, the characters in *Lord of the Flies* become allegorical agents through the correspondence of a state of nature with a state of mind. The more the boys stay on the island, the more they become aware of its sinister and actively hostile elements. The description of the pleasant Coral Island fantasy world quickly dissolves into images of darkness, hostility, danger. The boys accept "the pleasures of morning, the bright sun" and the unrestricted play, but by afternoon the overpowering sunlight becomes "a blow that they ducked" (p. 65). Though dusk partly relieves the situation, the boys are then menaced by the dark: "When the sun sank, darkness dropped on the island like an extinguisher and soon the shelters were full of restlessness, under the remote stars" (p. 66).

The boys' attitude of childish abandon and romantic adventure changes to a much more sober one when the possibility of a beast is introduced. At that point the island is transformed into a dark haven for unspeakable terrors. The boys' increasing appre-

hension about their immediate physical safety parallels the gradual awareness that is taking shape in the minds of Simon, Piggy,
and particularly Ralph, concerning the *real* evil of the island. The
boys mistakenly project their own bestiality on an imaginary animal roaming the island, but Simon hesitantly speculates, "maybe
it's only us" (p. 103). The others do not understand. They look
into the blackened jungle for signs of the beast's movement. The
darkness is "full of claws, full of the awful unknown and menace"
(p. 116). Simon's inner vision, however, tells him that it is the
human being who is "at once heroic and sick" (p. 121). When
Simon confronts the Lord of the Flies, the pig's head on a stick,
it tells him (but really he tells himself), "Fancy thinking the Beast
was something you could hunt and kill! . . . You knew, didn't
you? I'm part of you?" (p. 172). The hostile island and its dark
mysteries are only a symbolic backdrop reinforcing the images
of savagery, bestiality, and destruction that describe, and reveal,
the boys themselves.

A third method by which the characters assume allegorical
significance is through the implicit comparison of an action with
an extrafictional event. James Baker was the first to point out similarities between Euripides' *The Bacchae* and Golding's novel.
The mistaken slaying of Simon recalls Pentheus's murder at the
hands of the crazed bacchantes of Dionysus. Pentheus's pride and
his inability to recognize Dionysus's powers lead to his downfall:
"This same lesson in humility is meted out to the schoolboys of
Lord of the Flies. In their innocent pride they attempt to impose
a rational order or pattern upon the vital chaos of their own nature. . . . The penalties (as in the play) are bloodshed, guilt, utter
defeat of reason."[9]

Both the novel and the play contain a beast-god cult, a hunt
sequence, and the dismemberment of the scapegoat figure.[10]
Though Simon is the clearest equivalent for Pentheus, Piggy and
finally Ralph are cast in similar roles. Piggy is destroyed, though
not dismembered, by Jack's forces. Ralph is chased by frenzied
hunters but is "saved" (by a deus ex machina process similar to
that of the end of Euripides' play) from the prospect of behead-
ing. Ralph fittingly becomes Golding's version of Agave. The boy,

like Pentheus's mother, mistakenly takes part in a killing and then must live sorrowfully with the knowledge of his, and all humanity's, capacity for blind destruction.

The actions that help establish parallels to religious events emphasize biblical analogues. Ralph's first blowing of the conch, proclaiming survival after the crash on the island, recalls the angel Gabriel's announcing good news. Inasmuch as the boys' "survival" is quite tentative, however, the implied comparison to Gabriel is ironic. Simon's fasting, helping the little boys, meditating in the wilderness, going up on the mountain—all these actions solidify the Christ parallel. The recurring pattern of falls—the falling parachutist, Piggy's fall to his death, the destruction of the conch in the same fall, Ralph's tumbling panic at the end of the novel—emphasizes the fall of humankind motif.

The extrafictional events pertaining to classical mythology or to Christ's passion enlarge the surface action with additional symbolic meanings.

The fourth and final technique for intensifying allegorical agents concerns the manifestation in an action of a state of mind. In *Lord of the Flies* a series of hunts, for either pigs or humans, symbolically demonstrates the boys' gradual deterioration into savages. Moral order is corrupted and the end result is chaos. William Mueller has established convincingly that "the book is a carefully structured work of art whose organization—in terms of a series of hunts—serves to reveal with progressive clarity man's essential core."[11] Mueller identifies six "hunts," but there are at least nine separate instances where this symbolic act occurs: (1) the first piglet, "caught in a curtain of creepers," escapes when Jack is mentally unable to kill the helpless creature (p. 32); (2) a second pig eludes the hunters, much to Jack's disgust (p. 55); (3) Jack is successful the next time, and the hunters conceive the ritual chant of "Kill the Pig. Cut her throat. Spill her blood" (p. 78); later Maurice briefly pretends to be the pig (p. 86); (4) during a mock ceremony that gets out of hand, Robert plays the role of the pig, in a scene that sinisterly foreshadows the transition from nonhuman to human prey (pp. 135–36); (5) after another successful hunt, the boys smear themselves with animal blood, and Maurice plays the pig while Robert ritually pokes him with a spear, to the delight of Jacks's hunters (pp. 161–63); (6) Jack and Roger play hunter and pig respectively, as Piggy and Ralph "find themselves eager to take a place in this demented but partly secure society" (p. 181); (7) Simon is mistaken for the beast and is torn to pieces; (8) Piggy is killed by Roger, who acts "with a sense of delirious abandonment" (p. 216); (9) and finally Ralph is the object of the last murderous hunt.

THE TWO fundamental patterns by which allegorical action is resolved are those of "progress" and "battle." The journey motif is first established by the plot circumstances of the opening chapter. A group of boys has been taken by airplane from a war-threatened England to a safer territory, but in the process their plane is attacked and they have been dropped to safety on a deserted island. Their thwarted flight is mentioned in the opening exposition. Though their physical, outer journey has ended, they soon begin a more recondite "journey." Through their quest for the beast, they (or at least Simon and Ralph) discover the real beast, humanity's own predilection for evil.

The structure of *Lord of the Flies* provides for a gradual revelation of insight, as Ralph sees his friends slowly turn into beasts themselves. The significance of the final scene, in which the naval officer reestablishes an adult perspective, is not what James Gindin once contended: "a means of cutting down or softening the implications built up within the structure of the boys' society on the island."[12] The officer's presence does not reaffirm that "adult sanity really exists," nor is it merely a gimmick that "palliates the force and the unity of the original metaphor."[13] On the contrary, it provides the final ironic comment: Ralph is "saved" by a soldier of war, a soldier who cannot see that the boys have symbolically reenacted the plight of all persons who call themselves civilized and yet continue to destroy their fellow humans in the same breath.

The irony of this last scene is consistent with Golding's sarcastic treatment of Ballantyne, and it also emphasizes the universality of Ralph's experience. There is no distinction between child and adult here. The boys' ordeal is a metaphor for the human predicament. Ralph's progress toward self-knowledge culminates in his tears: "Ralph wept for the end of innocence, the darkness of man's heart, and the fall through the air of the true, wise friend called Piggy" (p. 242). Because Piggy represents the failure of reason, the use of "wise" offers a further irony.

The battle motif is developed in both physical confrontations and rhetorical "combat." Initially, the pig hunts are ritualized tests of strength and manhood, but when the hunters eventually seek human prey (Simon, Piggy, and finally Ralph) the conflict is between the savage and the civilized; blind emotion and prudent rationality; inhumanity and humanity; evil and good. This conflict is further established in the chapter entitled "The Shell and the Glasses," when Jack's hunters attack Ralph's boys and steal Piggy's glasses. Jack carries the broken spectacles— which have become symbolic of intellect, rationality, and civilization—as ritual proof of his manhood and his power over his enemies: "He was a chief now in truth; and he made stabbing motions with his spear" (p. 201). In the "Castle Rock" chapter, Ralph opposes Jack in what is called a "crisis" situation: "They met with a jolt and bounced apart. Jack swung with his fist at Ralph and caught him on the ear. Ralph hit Jack in the stomach and made him grunt. Then they were facing each other again, panting and furious, but unnerved by each other's ferocity. They became aware of the noise that was the background to this fight, the steady shrill cheering of the tribe behind them" (p. 215).

More subtle forms of "battle"—debate and dialogue—are dramatized in the verbal exchanges between Jack and Ralph. Golding emphasizes their polarity: "They walked along, two continents of experience and feeling, unable to communicate" (p. 62). Later when Jack paints his face and flaunts his bloodied knife, the conflict is heightened: "The two boys faced each other. There was the brilliant world of hunting, tactics, fierce exhilaration, skill; and there was the world of longing and baffled commonsense" (p. 81). When Ralph does not move, Jack and the others have to build their fire in a less ideal place: "By the time the pile [of firewood] was built, they were on different sides of a high barrier" (p. 83). Different sides of the wood, different continents, different worlds—all these scenes intensify the symbolic as well as physical conflict. Here we encounter "a structural principle that becomes Golding's hallmark: a polarity expressed in terms of a moral tension. Thus, there is the rational (the firewatchers) pitted against the irrational (the hunters)."[14]

In both chapter 2, "Beast from Water," and chapter 8, "Gift for the Darkness," the exchange of views about whether there is a beast or not "becomes a blatant allegory in which each spokesman caricatures the position he defends."[15] Ralph and Piggy think that rules and organization can cure social ills, and that if things "break up," it is because individuals are not remembering that life "is scientific," rational, logical (p. 97). Jack hates rules, only wishes to hunt, and believes that evil is a mystical, living power that can be appeased by ritual sacrifice (p. 159). Simon feels that evil is not outside but rather within all human beings, though he is "inarticulate in his effort to express mankind's essential illness" (p. 103). He uses comparisons with excrement and filth to describe his notion of human inner evil.

Simon's confrontation with the pig's head on a stick, the Lord of the Flies, is another instance of allegorical dialogue. At first, Beelzebub seems to triumph: Simon is mesmerized by the grinning face (p. 165); he is warned that he is "not wanted," for Simon is the only boy who possesses a true vision of the nature of evil; and finally he faints (p. 172). However, Simon recovers, asks himself, "What else is there to do?" (p. 174), discovers the dead parachutist, and then takes the news about the "beast" to the rest of the boys. The entire scene with the pig's head represents the conflict that is occurring within Simon's own consciousness. The Lord of the Flies is only an externalization of the inner evil in all humans. Later when Ralph comes upon the pig's head, "the skull [stares at] Ralph like one who knows all the answers and won't tell" (p. 22). Though Ralph does not understand the significance of the pig, he does feel a "sick fear." In desperation he hits the head, as if breaking it would destroy the evil on the island. However, the broken pig's head lies in two pieces, "its grin now six feet across" (p. 222). Rather than being destroyed, it ironically has grown. In the final pages of the novel, when Ralph is desperately fleeing from the hunters, he runs in circles and retraces his steps back to the broken pig's head, and this time its "fathom-wide grin" entirely dominates the burning island.

FOUR PATTERNS of imagery reinforce the symbolism in *Lord of the Flies*. Images pertaining to excrement, darkness, falling, and animalism help define the human capacity for evil and savagery.

The many references to excrement, and also to dirt, underline thematically the vileness of human nature itself. As the boys' attempts at a sanitation program gradually break down, the inherent evil in human nature is symbolically manifested in the increasing images that refer to dung: "the two concepts merge in Golding's imagination—covertly in *Lord of the Flies* and manifestly in *Free Fall,* which is a literary cloaca, full of that revulsion psychologists try to explain in terms of the proximity and ambiguity of the apertures utilized for birth and excreta."[16]

Images associated with excrement (and more generally, dirt) are used in a negative sense, depicting human corruption. The conch makes "a low, farting noise" (p. 15). Johnny, the first "littlun" Ralph and Piggy meet, is in the act of defecating (p. 16). Pig droppings are closely examined by Jack's hunters to determine how recently the pig has left a particular place; the temperature of feces has become the central subject of interest (pp. 54 and 132). Ralph slowly loses his battle against filth: "With a convulsion of the mind, Ralph discovered dirt and decay, understood how much he disliked [his own long, dirty hair]" (p. 88). Even when Piggy tries to clean his glasses, the attempt is in vain (p. 11). He is appalled at the increasing filth on the island: "'We chose those rocks right along beyond the bathing pool as a lavatory. . . . Now people seem to use anywhere. Even near the shelters and the platform. You littluns, when you're getting fruit; if you're taken short—' The assembly roared. 'I said if you're taken short you keep away from the fruit. That's dirty'" (p. 92).

Weekes and Gregor recognize the realistic level of description here—eating nothing but fruit does indeed bring on diarrhea—but they add, "The diarrhea might seem to invite allegorical translation—the body of man is no longer fit for Eden."[17] At one significant point, the inarticulate Simon tries to think of "the dirtiest thing there is" (p. 103) in order to describe the fallen human condition, and Jack's answer, "one crude expressive syllable," reaffirms the metaphor of excrement, which prevails throughout the novel. The area near the decaying, fallen parachutist is "a rotten place" (p. 125). When the pig's head is mounted on the stick, it soon draws a "black blob of flies"; it is literally a lord of the flies, as well as figuratively Beelzebub, from the Hebrew *baalzebub,* "lord of flies." Sometimes this name is translated "lord of dung." By the end of the novel, Ralph himself has been reduced to a dirty, piglike animal.

Golding uses light-dark contrasts in a traditional way: the numerous images of darkness underline the moral blackness of the boys' crumbling society. The normal associations with the sinister, with death, with chaos, with evil are suggested by this imagery. Decaying coconuts lie "skull-like" amid green shadows (p. 7); Jack's choirboys are clothed in black; the beast is naturally associated with the coming of night (p. 39); the "unfriendly side of the mountain" is shrouded in hushed darkness (p. 48). Roger is described as a dark figure: "the shock of black hair, down his nape and low on his forehead, seemed to suit his gloomy face and make what had seemed at first an unsociable remoteness into something forbidding" (p. 68).

With a Hawthornesque touch, Golding describes the subtle change that has come over all the boys' faces, after the group has become largely a hunting society: "faces cleaned fairly well by the process of eating and sweating but marked in the less accessible angles with a kind of shadow" (p. 130). Jack is described as "a stain in the darkness" (p. 142). Generally, the coming of night turns common surroundings into a nightmare landscape of imaginary horrors: "The skirts of the forest and the scar were familiar, near the conch and the shelters and sufficiently friendly in daylight. What they might become in darkness nobody cared to think" (p. 155).

Images of light and brightness are identified with spirit, regeneration, life, goodness. The description of Simon's dead body as it is carried out to sea suggests transcendence: "Softly, surrounded by a fringe of inquisitive bright creatures, itself a silver shape beneath the steadfast constellations, Simon's dead body moved out toward the open sea" (p. 184). The contrast between the bright, gaudy butterflies and the black flies on the pig's head emphasizes the symbolic conflict between good and evil used throughout the novel. The bright butterflies are drawn to the sun-

light and to open places (p. 64); they surround the saintly Simon
(p. 158); they are oblivious to the brutal killing of the sow: "the
butterflies still danced, preoccupied in the centre of the clearing"
(p. 162). In this particular instance, they remind the reader of
those indifferent seagulls in Stephen Crane's "The Open Boat"—
simply a part of nature, not threatened by the environment, and
a mocking contrast to the violent predicaments that human beings either perpetuate or suffer. But the butterflies represent a
more positive force, and significantly they desert the open space
dominated by the grinning pig's head.[18]

Golding's obsession with the fallen human state permeates
the imagery of *Lord of the Flies.* The opening chapter is typical.
Ralph appears amid a background of fallen trees. He trips over
a branch and comes "down with a crash" (p. 5). He talks with
Piggy about coming down in the capsule that was dropped from
the plane. He falls down again when attempting to stand on his
head (p. 25). He pretends to knock Simon down (p. 28). In addition to the descriptions of the fallen parachutist, Simon's fainting
spells, Ralph's "nightmares of falling and death" (p. 229), and his
final collapse at the feet of the naval officer, the act of falling is
closely associated with the idea of lost innocence. Ralph weeps
for "the end of innocence . . . and the fall through the air" of
Piggy.

Animal imagery reinforces the boys' transformation into savages and subhumans. Predictably, evil is associated with the
beast, the pig's head, or a snake, but as the story progresses, the
boys themselves are described with an increasing number of animal images.

The boys' disrobing early in the novel at first suggests a return to innocence, but as the hunters become more and more
savage, their nakedness merely underscores their animalism.
Sam and Eric grin and pant at Ralph "like dogs" (pp. 17 and 46).
Jack moves on all fours, "dog-like," when tracking the pig (p. 53);
during the hunt he hisses like a snake, and is "less a hunter than
a furtive thing, ape-like among the tangle of trees" (p. 54). Ralph
calls him a "beast" (p. 214). Piggy, whose very name suggests an
obvious comparison, sees that the boys are becoming animals;
he says that if Ralph does not blow the conch for an assembly,

"we'll soon be animals anyway" (p. 107). Without his glasses, Piggy laments that he will "have to be led like a dog" (p. 204). When he dies, his body twitches "like a pig's after it has been killed" (p. 217). Simon, hidden in the shadows of the forest, is transformed into a "thing," a "beast," when the narration shifts to the other boys' view (pp. 182–83).

Ralph's transformation is slower than the others, but it is clearly discernible. Early in the novel, he viciously accepts the hunters' raw pig meat and gnaws on it "like a wolf" (p. 84). He is caught up in the savage ritual when Roger plays the pig (p. 181); he is part of the unthinking gang that murders Simon. When Piggy is killed, Ralph runs for his life and obeys "an instinct that he did not know he possessed" (p. 217). In the last chapter, Ralph is little more than a cornered animal. Ironically he sharpens a stick in self-defense and becomes a murderous hunter himself: "Whoever tried [to harm him] would be stuck, squealing like a pig" (p. 231). We are told that he "raised his spear, snarled a little, and waited" (p. 233). Ralph's transformation is both shocking and saddening. Alone in the forest, he brutally attacks the first adversary he meets: "Ralph launched himself like a cat; stabbed, snarling, with the spear, and the savage doubled up" (p. 234). When Ralph is trapped in the underbrush, he wonders what a pig would do, for he is in the same position (p. 236).

Related to these animal images is the continual reference to the word *savage*. In *Lord of the Flies* the distinction between civilized human being and savage becomes increasingly cloudy and a source of further irony. Early in the novel Jack himself proclaims, "I agree with Ralph. We've got to have rules and obey them. After all, we're not savages" (p. 47). Piggy asks more than once, "What are we? Humans? Or animals? Or savages?" followed by the double irony, "What's grownups going to think?" (p. 105). The painted faces of the hunters provide "the liberation into savagery" (p. 206), an ironic freedom to destroy society; and the animal imagery contributes to this idea.

SEVERAL "levels" of meaning operate in *Lord of the Flies,* apart from the surface narrative. First, from a particular psychological viewpoint, the tripartite organization of the human psyche—ego, id, superego—is dramatized symbolically in the characters of Ralph, Jack, and Piggy, respectively. The conflict between Ralph, the level-headed elected leader of the boys' council, and Jack, the self-appointed head of the hunters, corresponds to an ego-id polarity. Ralph realistically confronts the problem of survival and works out a practical plan for rescue. Jack is quick to revert to savagery, dishonesty, violence. Piggy, the fat, bespectacled rationalist, reminds Ralph of his responsibilities, makes judgments about Jack's guilt, and generally represents the ethical voice on the island. Since Piggy does not acknowledge his own share of guilt for Simon's death, Oldsey and Weintraub conclude that this inconsistency "spoils the picture often given of Piggy as superego or conscience."[19] However, the many times Piggy reminds the weakening Ralph of what must be done far outweigh this one reversal.

A second level of symbolism emerges from the archetypal patterns in the novel. The quest motif is represented by Ralph's stumbling attempts at self-knowledge. His is literally an initiation by fire. Ironically the knowledge he acquires does not allow him to become an integrated member of adult society, but rather it causes him to recoil from the nightmare world he discovers. He is a scapegoat figure who must be sacrificed as atonement for the boys' evils. Simon and Piggy are also variants of the scapegoat symbol. Simon is most clearly the saint or Christ figure. The Dionysian myth is also reworked, as the boys' blindness to their own irrational natures leads to their destruction. As James Baker has observed, Euripides' *Bacchae* "is a bitter allegory" of not only the degeneration of society but also of essential human blindness: "the failure of rational man who invariably undertakes the blind ritual-hunt in which he seeks to kill the threatening 'beast' within his own being."[20]

On still another level, *Lord of the Flies* accommodates a political allegory in which Ralph represents democracy and Jack totalitarianism. Golding has often stressed the impact of World War II on his own life and his change from an idealist who believed in human perfectibility, to a more skeptical observer who had discovered a dark truth "about the given nature of man."[21] In his most explicit statement about the effect of the war on his estimation of humanity and its political systems, Golding says:

> It is bad enough to say that so many Jews were exterminated in this way and that, so many people liquidated—lovely, elegant word—but there were things done during that period from which I still have to avert my mind lest I should be physically sick. They were not done by the headhunters of New Guinea, or by some primitive tribe in the Amazon. They were done, skillfully, coldly, by educated men, doctors, lawyers, by men with a tradition of civilization behind them, to beings of their own kind. . . . When these destructive capacities emerged into action they were thought aberrant. Social systems, political systems were composed, detached from the real nature of man. They were what one might call political symphonies. They would perfect most men, and at the least, reduce aberrance.
>
> Why, then, have they never worked?[22]

Such statements not only define Golding's own social background but also illuminate his use of the microcosmic island society in *Lord of the Flies*.

Golding's own comments about *Lord of the Flies* continually focus on the potentials and the limitations of the democratic ideal. Though he supports a democratic doctrine, he recognizes its weaknesses: "You can't give people freedom without weakening society as an implement of war, if you like, and so this is very much like sheep among wolves. It's not a question with me as to whether democracy is the right way so much, as to whether democracy can survive and remain what it is."[23] By giving up all its principles, the island society of *Lord of the Flies* demonstrates the inefficacy of political organizations that attempt to check human beings' worst destructive instincts. It is only by first recognizing these dark powers that democracy can hope to control them.

The fourth level of meaning is the moral allegory, which focuses on the conflicts between good and evil, and encourages philosophical or theological interpretations. Golding is defining the nature of evil. Whether it is embodied in a destructive, unconscious force, a mistaken sacrifice that unsuccessfully atones for the boys' collective guilt, or a dictatorial power opposing the democratic order (corresponding to the psychological, archetypal, and politico-sociological levels, respectively), the problems of moral choice, the inevitability of original sin and human fallibility, the blindness of self-deception create a fourth level of meaning in the novel.

The island is not only a stage on which characters must make crucial moral decisions but also a microcosm for the human mind, in which ethical conflicts similarly occur. Because Golding believes that "a fabulist is always a moralist," he assigns a significant pattern of imagery to Ralph, "the fair boy" (p. 5), who unties the "snake-clasp of his belt" (p. 7). Ralph possesses a "mildness about his mouth and eyes that proclaims no devil" (p. 7); he rallies the boys to the open, sunlit part of the island; his conch sounds a Gabriellike note unifying (if only temporarily) his followers. Jack, on the other hand, is identified with darkness and violence: when his band of choirboys first appears, it is described as "something dark," like a "creature" (p. 19); the black caps and cloaks hide their faces; Jack's red hair suggests a devilish element; his impulsive decision to be a hunter and kill pigs foreshadows his demonic monomania for destruction; when he first meets Ralph, Jack is sun-blinded after coming out of the dark jungle.

However, because Golding complicates the characterization and shows Ralph to be susceptible to evil forces and at times paradoxically sympathetic to Jack, the reader recognizes ambiguities not easily compatible with a neat but rigid system of symbols. If *Lord of the Flies* "teaches" through its moral allegory, it is the lesson of self-awareness: "The novel is the parable of fallen man. But it does not close the door on that man; it entreats him to know himself and his Adversary, for he cannot do combat against an unrecognized force, especially when it lies within him."[24]

3   *The Inheritors*

The Inheritors, Golding's second novel, has much in common with *Lord of the Flies*. Both novels explore the nature of evil, and both consider the close relationship between intelligence and evil. The presumably intelligent schoolboys opt for savagery and human destruction. The innocent Neanderthals of *The Inheritors* are annihilated by the "superior" race of Homo sapiens, whose increased intelligence only makes them more proficient murderers. Golding observes that "the quality of innocence in Neanderthal man is a very sad thing, inseparable from ignorance; whereas, perhaps, in boys [i.e., in *Lord of the Flies*] intelligence and evil are not inseparable, but parallel things, as a matter of genetics."[1]

Both novels also contain isolated settings as part of their allegorical method. Much of the action in *The Inheritors* occurs on an island bordered on one side by a raging waterfall. But Golding has isolated his characters in time as well as space. His second novel is set in prehistory, at the very dawn of humankind, as the Neanderthals first encounter modern beings. This atmosphere of timelessness is characteristic of Golding's work. His novels contain either extensive flashback (*Pincher Martin, Free Fall, The Pyramid*) or establish isolated settings in earlier times (*The Inheritors, The Spire*).

The Inheritors is told from the severely limited point of view of Lok, a subhuman primitive who is unable to rationalize and whose crude attempts at thinking are announced by "I have a picture." Because of Golding's technical achievement in manipulating point of view and language, reminiscent of Faulkner's handling of the Benjy section in *The Sound and the Fury,* numerous critics have acclaimed *The Inheritors* a tour de force.[2] Many, on the other hand, have called it muddled, over abstract, or deliberately baffling.[3] As with *Lord of the Flies,* the theme of *The Inheritors* is more profound than merely a lament for lost innocence. Like the first novel, *The Inheritors* is developed through allegory. The theme is thrown into clearer focus by an abrupt change in viewpoint, occurring in the final chapter, just as the appearance of the naval officer at the end of *Lord of the Flies* had increased the impact of Golding's ironic *Coral Island* motif and had also shown that the boys' catastrophe was a metaphor for a worldwide predicament.

In the manner that Golding's first novel reacted to Ballantyne's *Coral Island, The Inheritors* offers a contrasting version of H. G. Wells's *The Outline of History.*[4] The epigraph to Golding's novel is taken directly from *The Outline,* in which Wells characterizes Neanderthals with the words "ugliness," "repulsive strangeness," "inferior stature," and then quotes from Sir Harry Johnston: "The dim racial remembrance of such *gorilla-like monsters,* with cunning brains, shambling gait, hairy bodies, strong teeth, and possibly *cannibalistic tendencies,* may be the germ of the *ogre* [all italics added] in folklore."[5] In a passage preceding the one quoted by Golding, Wells had discussed the way Homo sapiens or "the true men," as he calls them, had dispossessed *Homo neanderthalensis,* driving them out of their caverns and quarries. Wells optimistically proclaims, "the appearance of [Homo sapiens] was certainly an enormous leap forward in the history of mankind."[6]

Golding objects to this tidy rationalistic philosophy of progress and evolutionary superiority. He states that *The Outline* "played a great part in my life because my father was a rationalist, and the *Outline* . . . was something he took neat."[7] But Golding was not content with Wells's pat optimism: *The Outline* "seemed to me to be too neat and slick. And when I re-read it as an adult I came across his picture of Neanderthal man, our immediate predecessors, as being the gross brutal creatures who were possibly the basis of the mythological bad man, whatever he may be, the ogre. I thought to myself that this is just absurd. What we're doing is externalising our own inside."[8] The "Beast" in *Lord of the Flies* is clearly one such externalization of "our own inside."

The Inheritors provides a more complicated view of human-kind than does Wells's *The Outline,* and suggests that the human potential for evil accompanies whatever social, moral, or intellectual progress we might achieve. Our capacity for self-destruction, or the destruction of others, partially defines what it is to be human. As Golding has observed, "It's an odd thing—as far back as we can go in history we find that the two signs of Man are a capacity to kill and a belief in God."[9] *The Inheritors,* like all of Golding's novels, offers the reader much more, however, than dark pessimism.

THE PERSONIFIED agents in *The Inheritors* are first developed by no-menclature. The proper names not only reflect abstract qualities of the characters, but also reemphasize the Wellsian precedents for Golding's novel. Besides using *The Outline of History* as a background source that expands the meaning of *The Inheritors,* Golding draws on short stories by Wells. In "The Grisly Folk,"[10] "The Monkey People,"[11] and "A Story of the Stone Age"[12]—all sources for Golding—Homo sapiens emerges as a victorious, superior creature; by contrast, Neanderthals are portrayed as subhuman gorillas. The simple proper names used in *The Inheritors*—some names evolving from natural, physical features that the character possesses—point to an earlier work by Wells. The names in "A Story of the Stone Age" (Wau, Uya, Cat's-skin, One-eye, Snail-eater, Snake) are similar to Golding's character names (Lok, Liku, Pine-tree, Chestnut-head, Bush, Tuft). The simplicity of the names is consistent with the crudeness of the characters' language and mentality. Golding's epigraph from *The Outline,* his admitted knowledge of Wells's short stories, and even the similarities in the names for his primitive characters, suggest that Golding is fashioning a revised version of Wells's thesis. The references to Wells, both direct and indirect, contribute to Golding's irony.

Besides recalling similarities to "A Story of the Stone Age," the names of Golding's fictional cave dwellers imply specific qualities of characterization. Golding's allegory offers what has been called "an anthropological version of the Fall of Man,"[13] and the contrast between the innocent Neanderthals and the more corrupt Homo sapiens is reflected even in their personal names. For example, "Liku," the name for the happy little girl stolen by the new persons suggests "like you," while Liku's counterpart in the Homo sapiens group is Tanakil, the idea of "kill" built into the last syllable. Not all connotations, however, always involve neat contrasts between good and evil. Mal, the Neanderthal old leader, is physically sick, as his name implies, and his death, early in the novel, signals the beginning of the end for the old order. "Fa" suggests "fall," which is the literal (and symbolic) fate of that character. Lok's limited mental powers "lock" his mind in ignorance throughout most of the narrative. The name "Marlan," given to the leader of the new people, "sounds like a combination of 'Mal' with Merlin, and this leader proves in fact to be an evil magician."[14] And though "Tuami"—"your friend"—is used ironically, it also sounds like "you are me," an idea appropriate to the end of the novel, when Tuami is shown to be not only an updated version of Lok (they both look into darkness and chaos) but also a representation of all modern human beings, and consequently a character with whom the reader must sympathize.

A second analogy, the correspondence of a state of nature with a state of mind, is developed in three ways. First, the primitive forest corresponds with the innocent, Edenlike existence of the Neanderthals. The forest, up to the time at which the novel begins, has been kind to the primitives. They all remember "when it was summer all year round the flowers and fruit hung on the same branch."[15] Second, the unknown territory of the island is equated with fear and foreboding. The very atmosphere seems to threaten the Neanderthals (and, of course, when they finally encounter Homo sapiens, their fears are confirmed). The swirling waters, separating the island from the Neanderthals, are tempestuous, dangerous, evil (p. 41). The hidden eyes of the is- land cliffs haunt Lok's mind. When Lok and Fa, his mate, return from the island territory without finding Ha (the first Neanderthal who is killed by the new people), they feel as if some unseen evil is stalking them: "As if the terror of the [forest] sanctuary was pursuing them, the two people broke into a run" (p. 86). To Lok, the water by the falls is a manifestation of evil and destruction, "a wilderness" of foaming power that shakes the very earth (p. 126). Third, the Neanderthals have come upon hard times (they have come too early to the spring camping grounds; past forest fires have reduced their numbers and their food supply; and they, unknowingly, are dangerously close to extermination at the hands of an unseen enemy), and just as they live on the brink of extinction and disaster, so the great forest fire that they discuss in fearful tones (p. 45) becomes a symbol of their impending fate.

At the beginning of chapter 5, after the Neanderthals have discovered that there are "others" on the island, the old woman, who has replaced the deceased Mal as leader of the group, says that the fear they are experiencing "is like when the fire flew away and ate up all the trees" (p. 93). At this point, even the forest birds communicate the general uneasiness: "birds began to cry and the sparrows dropped down" (p. 92). Still later, Fa uses the same symbol to characterize the new people who bring destruction: "they are like a fire in the forest" (p. 197).

Allusions to extrafictional events refer to biblical analogues, through which Golding creates new versions of old myths. Golding imaginatively reworks the Genesis motif, establishing an Edenlike setting in which the Neanderthals, as well as Homo sapi- ens, reenact the fall of humankind. The tree from which Lok and Fa observe the corrupt practices of the new people becomes a symbolic Tree of Knowledge, particularly for Fa, who witnesses the cannibalistic destruction of Liku. Fa shudders in disbelief, "as though the moonlight that fell on the tree were wintry" (p. 175); she feels the cold chill of a bitter knowledge. The scene in which Lok and Fa sample the new humans' liquor and subsequently become as brutal, selfish, and sadistic as their enemies (pp. 199–204) reaffirms the idea of their fall from innocence.

The waterfall is itself a symbol of the human Fall. Its roaring waters—"monstrous," "unending," "profound"—make human voices sound "puny and without resonance" (p. 195). When Fa, with her newfound knowledge, is swept over the falls to her death, the action is enlarged symbolically. Knowledge of evil is associated with the water. When Lok says that the water is "a terrible thing," Fa sorrowfully adds, "the water is better than the new people" (p. 197). The dramatic fall of Chestnut-head over the cliff to his death, "leaving not even a scream behind him" (p. 211), reiterates the Fall motif.

The manifestation in an action of a state of mind is embodied in the systematic destruction of the Neanderthals by Homo sapiens. As each member of the small group of Neanderthals disappears or is murdered, the terrifying depravity of the new people is revealed. Also with each death Lok becomes slightly more aware of the true nature of the new people. As the murders proliferate, Lok's innocence diminishes, until finally he is left alone in the darkness, crying over the bones of Liku.

The sequence of the seven Neanderthal deaths accounts for part of the suspense and narrative interest. First, Ha disappears in the vicinity of the island and is never heard of again (pp. 65–68). The death of Mal (p. 91), the last of the Neanderthal leaders, implies that the old, innocent order cannot survive much longer. The new people are even indirectly to blame for Mal's death, in that they have removed a log from across the water, and Mal falls into the river. As Fa says, "the log that wasn't there" killed Mal (p. 98). Lok discovers the old woman's dead body floating in the dark waters (pp. 108–9). Then young Liku and a baby simply called "the new one" are kidnapped (p. 105), while Nil is killed and thrown into the water (p. 114). Eventually Liku is killed and eaten by the cannibalistic Homo sapiens (p. 169). Fa, trying to escape the new people, is swept over the waterfalls to her death (p. 216). When the Homo sapiens depart with the "new one," Lok becomes the last Neanderthal, curls into a fetal position, and awaits death. The moment that Lok finally gains knowledge of human evil (his discovery of Liku's bones and the little "Oa" that she carried) coincides with the extinction of his race.

THE "PROGRESS" and "battle" motifs, characteristic of allegorical action, are introduced early in the novel. The problems the Neanderthals encounter as they migrate to their summer camping grounds foreshadow the impending defeat by Homo sapiens. Walter Sullivan observes that the "fall of the Neanderthals is two-fold. It is first moral, . . . then it is physical."[16] Their outer journey, thwarted by bad weather, difficult passage over the water, and the disappearance of Ha, parallels their imminent spiritual as well as physical destruction at the hands of the new people. The action in the novel develops a series of quests by the Neanderthals: the journey to the good lands; the hunt for the lost children; and most importantly, the attempts to discover who and what the "other" people are. It is this quest to *understand* that is "of desperate importance" (p. 76), and thus the physical efforts to find Homo sapiens are analogous to the spiritual journey toward knowledge of humankind, a journey that the reader accomplishes with more insight than does the dull-witted Lok.

When Golding shifts the point of view to Tuami in the last chapter, the same themes persist—the human struggle to know oneself, to live with one's own destructive powers, to make another beginning. Fittingly the story ends as the new people begin their own journey to the safer lands of another territory. That the kidnapped Neanderthal baby becomes a source of "love and fear" (p. 231) to Homo sapiens indicates that the new people too might hope to understand the "devils" they have just battled. The baby, then, is a symbol of both death and life, and a bridge between two races, between old and new, subhuman and human, innocence and corruption. The new people's contradictory feelings of fear and compassion for the child indicate the complexity of the forces in conflict here. The Homo sapiens are not total villains and, most significantly, Tuami's level of self-awareness, as he experiences the guilt and "irrational grief" (p. 225) of living in "a world of confusion" (p. 231), is the first step toward the Homo sapiens' insight into human nature—a nature that all human beings have inherited.

The battle motif in *The Inheritors* is developed via the characters' physical confrontations rather than through the use of rhetorical dialogue and debate, for the novel contains little "language" per se. The contrast between Neanderthal innocence and Homo sapiens destructiveness is intensified by these dramatic confrontations. When a Homo sapiens shoots at Lok with a poisoned arrow, the simple Neanderthal has "a confused idea that someone was trying to give him a present" (p. 111). Lok feels like laughing and does not realize that his very life is in danger.

The major physical conflict between the two races—when Lok unsuccessfully tries to retrieve Liku from the enemy camp while Fa creates a diversion—again illustrates Lok's ignorance. Instead of snatching the "new one" away from its captors, he merely asks Tanakil for Liku, unaware that Liku has been killed and eaten. The Homo sapiens cannibalism reveals what baseness the new people are capable of, and ironically reverses Wells's notion about the "cannibalistic tendencies" of the subhuman Neanderthals. Homo sapiens is the monster in Golding's novel.

Another significant variation of the battle motif is the Neanderthals' continual war with the hyenas. Lok identifies them with death and evil (p. 53), and his attempts to drive them away symbolically parallel his fight against death and extinction throughout the novel. The Neanderthals instinctively reach for stones when they sense the hyenas' presence (pp. 52, 123, 131). At the conclusion of the novel, when Lok is left to die, the hyenas wait nearby and then stealthily approach. The description that closes chapter 11 links together the "fall," the hyenas, and the symbolic breaking up of the ancient ice caps, signaling the end of the Neanderthal Age.

Though direct debate between the two groups of characters is minimized, the underlying structure of the novel is the series of contrasting scenes in which the Neanderthal is shown to be ironically more "human," in the best sense of that word, than Homo sapiens. The distinction that the Neanderthals make between themselves, the "people," and the new humans, the "other" (p. 71), is maintained to the end. James Baker notes that if an allegorist "is to achieve a lucid personification of attitudes, and so establish the stable symbolism on which fable depends, the purity or autonomy of each point of view must be maintained. The vital tensions and dialectics which sustain narrative interest must arise between . . . representative characters or tribes. . . .

We find in the *The Inheritors* the traits of each species frozen in a radical contrast which sustains the allegory."[17]

The contrasting scenes establish the polarity between the two groups. The new people use wet wood or green branches for their fires; the Neanderthals use dried firewood. When Lok sees the yellow smoke coming from the far side of the mountain, he laughs, for "no one but a fool or some creature too unacquainted with the nature of fire would use it so unwisely" (p. 57). The new people kill animals for meat; the Neanderthals eat only what they find in nature, largely a vegetarian diet. The Homo sapiens' shrill laughter is produced by drunkenness (p. 150); Lok's laughter is a natural sign of his good spirits. The new people think only of themselves (as shown by Vivani's vanity, Marlan's greed, Tuami's lust); the Neanderthals have a tightly knit social organization and depend on each other for the well-being of all. The new people's religion of blood sacrifice contrasts with the Neanderthals' quiet worship of Oa, goddess of earth and nature. Tuami and Vivani's lust is countered by Lok and Fa's empathy and simple love.

Baker believes that the dialectic established in *The Inheritors* threatens the illusion of reality, but such is not the case. The Neanderthals do not remain forever blind to the evils of Homo sapiens, nor are the new people the "completely depraved" creatures that Baker imagines them to be. Though Lok's gradual "insight" is admittedly limited, "hardly to be compared with Ralph's final epiphany on the beach,"[18] Tuami's intuition about his own evil and the "world of confusion" in which he lives is a significant revelation. The dramatic irony emanating from the limited viewpoints of both sets of characters adds a complexity to the novel that *Lord of the Flies* does not possess. Ralph eventually sees that the other boys merely externalized their own evil when they killed Simon or when they sacrificed the pig to the "beast."

In *The Inheritors*, Homo sapiens considers the Neanderthals to be "devils," and ironically flees from the helpless innocents whom they have in fact exterminated. Golding's novel requires a third view—the reader's—to establish the true perspective, a perspective that sees the continuity of the human predicament. Lok's total frustration, Tuami's uncertainty as he looks into the

darkness, the modern human situation as intellectual and techno-
logical advances outrun moral and social progress—all of these
difficulties, in Golding's view, characterize what it is to be human,
what it is to create and simultaneously to destroy. Golding does
not uniformly condemn Homo sapiens, nor does the novelist rel-
egate evil to any particular character.

FOUR PATTERNS of imagery also contribute to the symbolism in *The
Inheritors*. Images pertaining to darkness, falling, animalism, and
coldness reinforce the ideas of self-deception, evil, and savagery
specifically associated with the new humans, though at times applied to the Neanderthal group.

Images of darkness are identified with death, evil, and blind
ignorance (or self-deception). The connection between death
and evil is close, for it is Homo sapiens' evil that eventually obliterates the Neanderthals. The early death of Mal, the "darkness in
the air" surrounding the dead doe, the old woman's body floating
in the black waters—all signal the growing Neanderthal doom.
The recurring images of darkness associated with the "others"
and their island territory forebode evil. The land across the river
is a "dark wilderness" (p. 40), its cliffs obscured in shadows (p.
66). When Lok thinks about Ha's disappearance, he gazes into the
black distance beyond the Neanderthal campfire: "Out of the fire-
light everything was black and silver, black island, rocks and
trees. . . . All at once the night was very lonely and the picture
of Ha would not come back into his head" (p. 72). Lok's first encounter with the "other" is at night, and the new human he sees
is described as an indistinct "blob of darkness" (p. 79). Members
of Homo sapiens are "dark as the branches" (p. 101); their religious ceremonies are performed in the "dim light" of a night
camp fire (p. 129); after their drunken orgy, the new people
make "their way waist deep in shadows to separate caves"
(p. 178).

The confusion and uncertainty that Tuami feels, as the novel
shifts perspective in the last chapter, is symbolized by the world
of shadow and blackness that surrounds him. After escaping the
"devils," Tuami hopes "for the light as for a return to sanity" and
manhood. But the dawn changes nothing: "the world with the

boat moving so slowly at the centre was dark amid the light, was untidy, hopeless, dirty" (pp. 224–25). Tanakil, in reaction to the fate of her new friend, Liku, has gone mad, and Tuami can see "the night" in her dark, sunken eyes (p. 226). The new people's world of darkness is partly produced by their uneasy sense of guilt and sin. Tuami compares his feelings to the dark water that surrounds his boat: "I am like a pool, he thought, some tide has filled me, the sand is swirling, the waters are obscured and strange things are creeping out of the cracks and crannies in my mind" (p. 227). His futile attempt to see beyond the dark horizon ends the novel on an ironic note suggesting that Homo sapiens will live in just as much darkness as the "devils" who have just been fled. Marlan says that the devil Neanderthals "live in the darkness under the trees," yet the last paragraph of the novel describes the new people's similar predicament, specifically their own moral blindness in a world of chaos and shadow. Nevertheless, humanity must go on; it continues to travel forward, even into the face of the abyss: "Tuami looked at the line of darkness. It was far away and there was plenty of water in between. He peered forward past the sail to see what lay at the other end of the lake, but it was so long, and there was such a flashing from the water that he could not see if the line of darkness had an ending" (p. 233).

As in *Lord of the Flies,* images connected with falling predominate in *The Inheritors.* Every reference to the churning waters "eager to snatch [Lok's people] over the fall" (p. 41) foreshadows the Neanderthals' impending physical destruction at the hands of the already fallen new people. When Pine-tree's finger is chopped off during the Homo sapiens' sadistic religious ceremonies, Lok and Fa watch in silent terror. At that dramatic moment, the waterfall image is again introduced, symbolically emphasizing the new people's depraved state and signaling the growing knowledge of evil that threatens the Neanderthal innocence: "There was a great stillness so that the fall sounded nearer" (p. 147). A similar pattern of imagery occurs when the new people, after their drunken orgy, fall to the ground one by one (pp. 176–79); here they are literally as well as metaphorically the "people of the fall." The more Lok and Fa learn about the new people, the more they too are described with the same images of falling. Fearing for Liku and the Neanderthal baby, Lok and Fa desperately press together, "searching for a centre," and then fall to the ground (p. 131). Later, when Lok drinks the new people's liquor, his fall is both literal and figurative: "His eyes closed themselves and he fell down as over a cliff of sleep" (p. 204).

Animal imagery complements Golding's irony by symbolically emphasizing the Homo sapiens' savagery and viciousness. By contrast, the animal images describing the subhuman Neanderthals suggest natural innocence and gentleness.

The Neanderthals are usually compared to gentle, benign creatures. When Lok's people sense that Mal is dying, they wait, "still as deer at gaze" (p. 15). The "new one," oblivious to the old man's sickness, plays like a kitten (pp. 28 and 65). As Mal's condition becomes worse, his rapid breathing is like a doe's (p. 44). At times when Lok's silliness irritates Fa, she brushes at him "as at a fly" (p. 62). As Lok hunts for the "others," he leaps from branch to branch "like a red squirrel" (p. 103), and later Fa is described in the same manner (p. 207).

On the other hand, members of Homo sapiens are characterized by much harsher images. They are first compared to bears (pp. 79 and 95) and then to jungle cats. The scent of the "other" haunts the dark forest: "It was night and the scent had paws and a cat's teeth" (p. 93). When the innocent Liku is kidnapped, her scream sounds "like the noise the horse makes when the cat sinks its curved teeth into the neck and hangs there, sucking blood" (p. 105). Lok's encounter with Homo sapiens is more frightening than "when he had crouched on a rock with Ha and a cat had paced to and fro by a drained kill, looking up and wondering whether they were worth the trouble" (p. 141). Tuami's group is also compared to vile snakes (p. 187), foxes playing with helpless birds (p. 177), and beetles swarming over a dead bird (p. 214). The major image associated with the new people pertains to wolves (pp. 177, 183, 187). The new people are as "noisy as a pack of wolves in cry" (p. 170). Their sharp teeth are the "teeth that remembered wolf" (p. 174). Late in the novel, after Lok's knowledge of Homo sapiens has increased, he says, "The people [the new humans] are like a famished wolf in the hollow of a tree" (p. 195). In the final chapter, Marlan is ironically described as if *he* were a savage, red animal (p. 229) rather than the superior human being he professes to be. When he says the evil ones cannot follow them, he does not recognize the inherent evil that will always follow, for it is a part of him.

Images of coldness underline both the Neanderthals' creeping awareness of evil and the chilling intuition about their own extinction. Mal has brought his people to the summer lands too early, and consequently the Neanderthals must all take shelter from the cold (pp. 34 and 42). Mal is not sure that they can find food and, to Lok, "the knowledge that Mal had not been certain was like a cold wind" (p. 61). The uncertainty of the old man's leadership and the new threat from Homo sapiens make the Neanderthals' world a cold, menacing one. Lok's strange feelings of alienation and loneliness are expressed in a similar image: "He was cut off and no longer one of the people; as though his communion with the other had changed him he was different from them [his own people] and they could not see him. He had no words to formulate these thoughts but he felt his difference and invisibility as cold wind that blew on his skin" (p. 78). Upon Lok's first encounter with the "other" (p. 80), his hair rises and he shivers against both the cold weather and the chill of an unknown evil.

When Lok and Fa recognize that the new ones have powers of ingenuity far beyond the Neanderthals, Fa turns away, "shivering" in fear (p. 99). While watching Pine-tree lose a finger in the grotesque religious ceremony, Lok feels his skin tighten in a "wintry chill" (p. 146). After Fa witnesses the cannibalism, she shudders "suddenly as though the moonlight that fell on the tree were wintry" (p. 175). The Neanderthals, at the verge of extinction, understand that the new people have changed everything they have touched, sometimes for the better (as a result of their use of the wheel, their abilities at navigation, their spirit of adventure) but more often for the worse (because of their uncontrolled passion for destruction). Fa's simile expresses her people's fate with a fitting comparison: the new humans "have gone over us like a hollow log. They are like a winter" (p. 198).

THE IRONY in *The Inheritors* affects each of its "levels" of meaning—moral, psychological, mythic, and sociological. As a moral allegory, the novel reverses the Wellsian concept of the "superior" race subduing the Neanderthal subhumans: Golding's innocent Neanderthals offer a morality more desirable than that of Homo sapiens. However, the dichotomy is not so uniformly neat, for considerable sympathy is created for the new humans, whose struggle to understand themselves is focused in the last chapter. Similarly, the novel reverses any notion of an ego-id conflict, and the stereotyping of the Neanderthals as a representation of the dark, uncontrolled force of the id. Though Lok's people technically qualify as "irrational," their human warmth and sensitivity preclude the category of "ogres" from the id. The new humans are much more capable of wholesale destruction or undirected passion.

On a psychological level, then, the tension is more between the passive and active natures of all human beings: "Golding is not saying either state is preferable . . . but using his characters to indicate two sides of our nature which conflict: a tolerant side which is passive, and an active side that cannot fail to hurt."[19]

On the archetypal level, Golding is creating new myths (his own version of prehistory), which contain the timeless patterns of quest, initiation, the scapegoat, and primitive ritual. However, the new people's rituals strike the reader as ironically more "primitive" than those of Lok's people. Not only has Homo sapiens resorted to violence and human sacrifice, but it has superstitiously assumed that evil is external to itself. Consequently its world of totems (the symbol of the stag-robes; or the totem left to ward off devils) is fashioned by its own ignorance.

Finally, *The Inheritors* presents the sociological conflict between a tightly knit Neanderthal group, whose priority is unselfish human cooperation, and a Homo sapiens group, whose increased rationality has only produced debilitating self-interests and social disintegration. The dissension among the latter group is particularly evident in the last chapter, as Tuami plots Marlan's murder. The small band of new humans has been disenfranchised from a larger group when Marlan decided to steal Vivani, the wife of another. Now Tuami plans to steal Vivani from Marlan.

These new people have even stolen a Neanderthal baby from an alien society. In contrast, Lok's people cherish their social bonds. Their belief in human community and love expresses the ideals that Golding thinks are still vital to the human condition. Lok recognizes what the presence of the "other" is doing to his group: "The other had tugged at the strings that bound him to Fa and Mal and Liku and the rest of the people. The strings were not the ornament of life but its substance. If they broke, a man would die" (p. 78). Later in the novel Lok has the same picture: "And because he was one of the people, tied to them with a thousand invisible strings, his fear was for the people" (p. 104). His joy at seeing Fa again, after she has been separated from him, is genuine: "It is bad to be alone. It is very bad to be alone" (p. 196).

Ironically Homo sapiens will not admit to itself that uncontrolled selfishness leads to its own alienation. Lok considers the new people capable of wondrous miracles, yet essentially sick. Though he is frightened by them, he also feels "sorry for them as for a woman who has the sickness" (p. 193).

The title of the novel contains several ironies. The meek Neanderthals will *not* inherit the earth, and Homo sapiens will inherit (as do all humans) knowledge, and with it, the discovery of its devastating capacities for evil. However, *The Inheritors* is not just another instance of what has been called Golding's "antihumanism."[20] The novel implies that human awareness of its own nature is crucial to curbing its worst, most destructive, instincts. The reader discovers valuable insights to both Lok's world and, most importantly, Tuami's: "It is we who are the inheritors of *both*: most like the corrupt Tuami in the necessity of our sinfulness, but testifying to . . . our capacity for redemption by a greater span of perception and awareness. . . . Tuami could see no further [than the dark horizon], but we can, both technologically and intellectually, both physically and in the spiritual world which he allegorizes. . . . Weighted with Tuami, we strive for Lok."[21] Ironically, Golding's new people inherit a moral blindness that makes them externalize their own evil and then mistakenly exorcise self-made devils. A sad group of British schoolboys has shared the same inheritance.

Pincher Martin   4

Like Golding's first two novels, *Pincher Martin* combines the factual with the fabular, the mythic with the realistic, and contains a moral allegory portraying Martin's self-made purgatory. Golding's novel is not only an ironic version of the Prometheus myth but also a reaction to the predictable survival stories of Ballantyne and Defoe. The reader is first tempted to sympathize with Christopher Martin's painful struggle against the elements, but the novel makes it increasingly clear that its protagonist is an unethical, greedy egomaniac who is the cause of his own suffering. In the final chapter, the change in point of view, a device also common to Golding's first two novels, provides information (about Martin's true state) that has been carefully foreshadowed by the author.

The novel contains literary associations that make the narrative all the richer: "In the background of the novel the reader can recognize echoes . . . of Bierce ["An Occurrence at Owl Creek Bridge"] and of Hemingway ["The Snows of Kilimanjaro"], of Shakespeare's *Lear* [Pincher's "madness"] and Milton's Satan [particularly in Golding's opening chapter], of Eliot and of Conrad—and even of a minor adventure narrative of World War I entitled *Pincher Martin*."[1] But Golding's novel is more than merely a "denial of *Robinson Crusoe,*"² or a retelling of Ambrose Bierce. It questions the limits of free will: "What happens to somebody who exercises his free will and goes on exercising it? What's to be done?"³ Golding is "standing on its head"⁴ a theological concept concerning human freedom and is explaining the consequences of unchecked egoism. Thus the novel provides "an allegory of purgatorial experience."⁵ For its publication in the United States, the novel was renamed *The Two Deaths of Christopher Martin,* a title that supposedly would clarify the different levels of meaning: the survival story of the surface narration, and the deeper, eschatological implications of Pincher's war with God. Golding has commented on the symbolic meaning of his novel:

> Christopher Hadley Martin had no belief in anything but the importance of his own life, no God. Because he was created in the image of God he had a freedom of choice which he used to center the world on himself. He did not believe in purgatory and therefore when he died it was not presented to him in overtly theological terms. The greed for life which had been the mainspring of his nature forced him to refuse the selfless act of dying. . . . He is not fighting for bodily survival but for his continuing identity in face of what will smash it and sweep it away—the black lightning, the compassion of God. For Christopher, the Christ-bearer, has become Pincher Martin who is little but greed. Just to be Pincher is purgatory; to be Pincher for eternity is hell.⁶

The three allegorical levels in *Pincher Martin* concern one's physical struggle to stay alive in nature, the mental struggle to assert one's identity within a society, and to dominate other human beings, and the spiritual struggle to accept death.

The isolated setting is again part of Golding's allegorical method. After Martin's ship has been torpedoed, he finds himself cast upon a barren rock somewhere in the mid-Atlantic. At that moment, time stops for Christopher Martin. Because he is actually "suspended between life and death,"⁷ eternity itself is "there to be examined and experienced" (p. 14). The hours pass in what seems to be "an eternal rhythm" (p. 56); he watches the sun "for months without thought or identity" (p. 69) as time stretches on, indifferently (p. 182). His isolation is severe: "The darkness of separation was deeper than any living darkness because time had stopped or come to an end" (p. 168).

Christopher's conscious mind is described as a "center" or "globe," a little world unto itself (p. 48). His is a universal loneliness: "He became small, and globe larger until the burning extensions were interplanetary" (p. 49). The reader eventually discovers that the red silt and white rocks on the island are identical with Pincher's own blood and bones, and his own tongue and teeth. His entire world—which is now limited to the microcosmic island—is but a projection inside the teeth of his own skull. His feelings of separation and disorientation result from "his curious isolation inside the globe of his head" (p. 76).

Golding continually injects fragments of flashback to break down any notions of conventional clock time in the narrative. The transitions from present to past are unannounced and abrupt, contributing to the surrealistic flavor. The qualities of timelessness and isolation established in the opening chapters create the appropriate setting for Golding's allegory.

CHARACTER NAMES are important aspects of personification in *Pincher Martin*. The name "Pincher," besides being the nickname commonly given to any British sailor named Martin,[8] imagistically portrays the grasping, clawing nature of the man himself. His real name, "Christopher," literally means "Christ-bearer," and makes an ironic commentary on the protagonist, who egotistically tries to play God and also looks upon himself as a martyr to cruel fate (reinforcing, first, the ironic Christ-image and second, corresponding to the third-century Christian martyr of the same name). In addition, the initial sounds of *"Pincher Martin"* suggest a similarity to *"Prometheus,"* a figure to whom Martin also compares himself. Though Martin says, "I don't claim to be a hero" (p. 77), it is not long before he is declaring, "I am Atlas. I am Prometheus" (pp. 164, 189, 192), to the accompaniment of imaginary background music (pp. 164–65).

The parallels between the mythic Prometheus and Golding's

Pincher Martin are numerous: both defy God; both assert their will and intelligence against natural and supernatural forces; both are bound to a rock; both endure the agonies of prolonged suffering. But all these similarities are purposely transformed in Golding's work for the sake of irony. Prometheus defies a selfish, unjust God who has "grudged mortals the use of fire, and [is], in fact, contemplating their annihilation and the creation of a new race."[9] Prometheus defies God to champion humanity; Pincher defies God, but only to center the world upon himself, not for any heroic motive. Both characters use their intelligence to achieve their ends: Prometheus tricks Jupiter and steals fire for the benefit of humanity, but Pincher steals from everyone for the sole benefit of himself. Though both are bound to a rock, Prometheus is victimized by an angry God; Pincher suffers because he has made his own purgatorial rock as a consequence of his wicked life. Finally, Prometheus's suffering ends in triumph. He never relents and is eventually saved by Hercules. Though Pincher's last words are the defiant "I shit on your heaven!" (p. 200), he is slowly reduced to a pair of red claws, as he is defeated spiritually and physically.

Though many critics have responded sympathetically to Pincher's "Promethean" struggle,[10] Norman Podhoretz has most accurately described the discrepancy between Christopher's high estimate of his ability to survive and what he actually manages to do:

> Though he keeps reminding himself that he has intelligence and education to back up his unbounded will to live, though he identifies himself with Prometheus and Ajax, he never exhibits extraordinary resourcefulness. He forces anemones, mussels, and seaweed down his throat; he builds himself a shelter; he doctors an attack of food poisoning; he puts together makeshift signals out of stones and seaweed. Every one of these accomplishments is the product of a tremendous expenditure of will and a strenuous exertion of mind, and Mr. Golding means them to seem no less impressive than that. But under his subtle prompting we also begin to understand that they are, after all, elementary animal

achievements, that in themselves they are not enough to support Christopher Martin's conviction of the uniqueness and superiority of his humanity.[11]

Golding has little sympathy for Pincher: "In fact, I went out of my way to damn Pincher as much as I could by making him the nastiest type I could think of, and I was very interested to see how critics all over the place said, 'Well yes, we are like that.'"[12]

The names of other personified agents are appropriate. "Nathaniel," literally "God's gift," underlines that saintly character's goodness. Mary is the virgin whom Pincher attempts to seduce, as he egotistically plays the role of God. She also represents, with her surname Lovell, "the values which gave her life its quality (the unity of Mary and Lovewell),"[13] a quality that Pincher cannot understand. Even the name of the destroyer, *Wildebeeste,* suggests Pincher's own latent bestiality. The names of the plays in which he has acted, *Night Must Fall* and *The Way of the World,* make a symbolic comment on his own life and foreshadow his inevitable predicament.

In *Pincher Martin* the analogy between a state of nature and a state of mind is presented through the metaphor of the ruthless sea. Just as the sea is characterized as savage and openly hostile, so Martin is described as a brutal savage, fighting for his existence against an evil unseen force manifested in the unfriendly natural environment. Pincher attempts to dominate the elements just as he has dominated human beings in his sordid past. He opposes "the unavoidable fists of rock that beat him impersonally" (p. 42). The chill and the exhaustion become personified voices that tell him to give up (p. 45). Ironically he is now victim instead of victimizer. The voice that speaks from out of the black lightning personifies the antagonistic natural forces of which Pincher is acutely aware, while it also implies a metaphysical frame of reference that moves far beyond the natural world—a level of significance Pincher realizes only by the time the novel concludes. In addition to the raging sea and the voice from the black lightning, the inanimate stone Dwarf, which Pincher makes out of stacked rocks, becomes an ironic image of Christopher himself. The Dwarf made of stone symbolizes Martin's own hardness of heart. It is ironic that he looks closely at the blank stones in order to "find his face reflected there" (p. 107); the lifeless stones are indeed a reflection of his own barren soul.

Much of the action consistently corresponds with extrafictional events associated with classical mythology, specifically the Prometheus legend discussed above. One critic has also made a case for Pincher as "the lesser Ajax," who raped the virgin princess Cassandra, became shipwrecked on his journey from Troy, boasted that he saved himself without help from the gods, infuriated Poseidon, and was then killed by the angry god of the sea. Such a narrative of events parallels Martin's own life.[14] In addition, Golding's use of the classical theme of metamorphosis, as Pincher is gradually transformed into a pair of giant lobster claws, provides an appropriate moral judgment.

Biblical analogues are established through the absurd-saint motif. Not only does Christopher's name contribute to this theme, but also his sustained suffering (obviously not the result of his personal sacrifice) simulates Christ's passion. By the time he has stacked the large signal rocks into position, his hands are broken and he collapses in painful exhaustion (p. 62). Martin later attempts to play the very role of God. In a parody of the Creation, he names each of the sections of his island (p. 84), takes credit for making the rain ("let there be rain and there was rain," p. 171), and reverses the process by which humankind is created in God's image ("On the sixth day he created God. . . . In his own image created he Him," p. 196).

Recurrent patterns of action communicate the egotistic distortion of Pincher's mind and also symbolically comment on his spiritual condition. Martin's constant struggle to preserve his life, particularly his devouring of the mussels (pp. 66 and 74), parallels his own symbolic "devouring" of his fellow human beings. Christopher himself explains the significance of the "eating" metaphor: "And of course eating with the mouth was only the gross expression of what was a universal process. You could eat with your cock or with your fists, or with your voice. You could eat with hobnailed boots or buying and selling or marrying and begetting or cuckolding" (p. 88).

In his lifetime Pincher has lured Sybil away from Alfred, a

fellow actor; has seduced Helen, the wife of one of his producers; and has attempted to charm Mary, who eventually becomes Nathaniel's wife. When Pincher recalls his sexual conquests, he can only grin, "secure in his knowledge of the cosmic nature of eating" (p. 89). Consequently, as he thinks about "eating women, eating men, crunching up Alfred" (p. 90), his first impulse is to name the three prominent rocks on his island "the Teeth," but at the same moment he involuntarily shudders at the thought: "No! Not the Teeth!" He is unconsciously aware of the reality of his situation and therefore blanks out this terrible knowledge: "But to lie on a row of teeth in the middle of the sea—He began to think desperately about sleep" (p. 91).

Just as Pincher physically eats mussels on the rock (level one), and just as he figuratively eats persons in real life (level two), on a larger scale Pincher, as well as all human beings, is eaten by the universe, by life, by time. At this level, the book becomes an eschatological metaphor describing human progress from death to judgment to immortality. Though Pincher cannot accept the fact, he is not a god, but a man who must perform, in Golding's own words, "the selfless act of dying." John Peter, commenting on the nature of this universal process that obliterates Pincher, believes that the "bleakness of his [Pincher's] solitude offers no security against introspection and, as his selfishness comes to comprehend the self it serves, his personality disintegrates. Inexorably, as he has eaten others, the rocky teeth in the sea eat him."[15]

Early in the novel, Christopher defies the inevitability of death when he proclaims, "I'm damned if I'll die!" (p. 72), but he gradually perceives the futility of his egotism. He notices the rocks around him are like teeth: "They were the grinders of old age, worn away. A lifetime of the world had blunted them, was reducing them as they ground what food rocks eat" (p. 78). He eventually realizes that through death and the blackness of eternal sleep, "the carefully hoarded and enjoyed personality, our only treasure and at the same time our only defence, must die into the ultimate truth of things, the black lightning that splits and destroys all, the positive, unquestionable nothingness" (p. 91).

Thus, the abundance of "devouring teeth" images in *Pincher Martin* clearly supports the symbolic action.

Since Pincher is Greed personified, it is fitting that he is asked to play the role of Greed in one of his theater productions (pp. 118–20). Pincher's playing the part is a direct manifestation of his own state of mind. Peter, his producer, mockingly introduces Christopher to the part: "Chris-Greed. Greed-Chris. Know each other. . . . Let me make you two better acquainted. This painted bastard here takes anything he can lay his hands on. Not food, Chris, that's far too simple. He takes the best part, the best seat, the most money, the best notice, the best woman. He was born with his mouth and his flies open and both hands out to grab" (p. 120). The description is identical to Christopher, and Peter sarcastically adds, "Think you can play Martin, Greed?" The theme of Martin's greed generates the dominant metaphors of the novel: the maggot box, the lobster claws, the devouring teeth.

PINCHER MARTIN'S obvious outer quest is to effect a rescue (p. 81). He musters all his intelligence and education in an attempt to overcome the menacing environment and to devise a rescue plan. He builds the Dwarf, a stack of signal rocks; he wraps silver foil around the top rock, creating a crude reflector; he arranges seaweed in the form of a giant cross, which he hopes will be visible to passing aircraft. The cross image supports the theological implications of Martin's predicament, as well as depicting Pincher as an absurd Christ figure. But for Martin, neither physical nor spiritual rescue is forthcoming.

The action of the novel records Pincher's painful and unwilling pilgrimage to understand where he is and the significance of what has happened to him. When he is plotting Nat's murder in order to claim Mary for himself, Martin says that he is "chasing after—a kind of peace" (p. 105), also suggesting a sexual pun; dominating and destroying others is the only way he can bring order to his world. But Pincher's real pilgrimage is the journey to self-knowledge, accompanied by the realization that he is suspended in a purgatory of his own making.

As much as Pincher would deny it, all human beings "must

die into the ultimate truth of things." The novel presents the accumulating flashes of recognition that Martin cannot ignore: "I am shut inside my body. . . . How the hell is it that this rock is so familiar?" (pp. 124–25). The recurrent teeth imagery foreshadows his final realization that everything he experiences on the "rock" is really happening inside his own dead skull. Through a series of gradual revelations, Pincher comes to know not only where he is, but what he is. He unconsciously suspects, but will not admit, that he is dead: "I must have a beard pretty well. Bristles, anyway. Strange that bristles go on growing even when the rest of you is—" (p. 125). The familiarity of the rock haunts him: "There is something venomous about the hardness of this rock. It is harder than rock should be. And—familiar" (p. 129). At one point, Pincher quotes the military maxim, "Know your enemy" (p. 162), ironically spoken before he has recognized that his hellish rock is the symbolic consequence of his own evil existence. He is his own enemy. Though he denies the moral implications of his predicament ("All the terrors of hell can come down to nothing more than a stoppage. Why drag in good and evil when the serpent lies coiled in my own body?" p. 163), Pincher's "serpent" is more than a constipated intestine; it is the "bosom-serpent" of egotism, recalling the same image used in Hawthorne's tale.[16]

Pincher painfully copes with the emerging knowledge of his true state: "Something was coming up to the surface. It was uncertain of its identity because it had forgotten its name. It was disorganized in pieces. It struggled to get these pieces together because then it would know what it was. . . . It was a gap of not-being, a well opening out of world" (pp. 167–68). Martin only partially understands: "Then I was dead. That was death. I have been frightened to death. Now the pieces of me have come together and I am just alive." He later observes, "'Just when I was myself again and victorious, there came a sort of something. A Terror. There was a pattern emerging from circumstances.' Then the gap of not-being" (p. 169). Still his ego will not admit death, only "not-being."

By the end of chapter 11, Pincher has clearly discovered the connection between his rock island and the teeth of his own jar

(p. 174). More significant, however, is his realization, in the next chapter, that he himself is the cause of this terrible isolation. At this moment he achieves his most important insight: "Because of what I did I am an outsider and alone" (p. 181). His pilgrimage, unwilling as it is, has been accomplished. Pincher's self-made purgatory of egotism is crumbling: "Pincher has pursued the logic of a human universe to its absurd end, and has developed his selfhood to the point where it beckons toward the ultimate idiocy, where the outside world disappears and there is nothing but the unspeakable tedium of death [and] the quintessential nothingness."[17] The structure of *Pincher Martin* as moral allegory is clear. Golding sees his novel as "a straightforward morality. Pincher isn't a man really. He is Greed. That's why he's called Pincher. The book is a fairly objective exercise in trying to make out what happens to Greed when all the things that surround it and give it its food are taken away and it has nothing to prey on but itself."[18]

Consistent with the three levels of allegorical action—the physical, social, and spiritual struggles—are the three types of "battles" dramatized in *Pincher Martin*. Pincher's physical confrontations with a hostile environment are emphasized throughout the novel. At first, his battle against nature and his determined effort to endure create sympathy for him: "Another wave reached in and spray ran down his face. He began to labor at climbing. He moved up the intricate rock face until there were no more limpets nor mussels and nothing clung to the rock but his own body and tiny barnacles and green smears of weed. All the time the wind pushed him into the cleft and the sea made dispersed noises" (p. 34). The simple language (the preceding quoted passage contains only three words that are more than two syllables) is perfectly suited to Pincher's elemental struggle.

The sustained, emotionally detached descriptions (again comprised of one- and two-syllable words) of Pincher's laborious attempts to move only a few feet forward effectively communicate the torture of Martin's ordeal:

> Again he turned his face and looked up. His fingers closed over the limpet. Now his right leg was moving. The toes

searched tremulously for the first limpet as the fingers had
searched for the second. They did not find the limpet but
the knee did. The hand let go, came down to the knee and
lifted that part of the leg. The snarl behind the stiff face felt
the limpet as a pain in the crook of the knee. The teeth set.
The whole body began to wriggle; the hand went back to
the higher limpet and pulled. The man moved sideways up
the slope of the roof. The left leg came in and the seaboot
stocking pushed the first leg away. The side of the foot was
against the limpet. The leg straightened. Another torrent returned and washed down. (pp. 38–39)

Eventually Pincher makes his struggle take on cosmic proportions as he proudly imagines himself fighting "a hero's way from
trench to trench" (p. 192). The irony of such presumptuousness
has already been noted.

Apart from this elemental battle with nature are Pincher's
past battles with other persons. These physical confrontations are
presented in flashback throughout the novel: Martin's attempted
rape of Mary (p. 152); Peter's bicycle "accident," which Pincher
has arranged (p. 153); Martin's seduction of the producer's wife
(p. 153); his attempted murder of Nat (p. 186). Pincher's life has
been little more than a play for power, for domination, for the
control of other human lives in order to benefit his own monstrous ego. Though he has won more of these battles than he
has lost, he realizes that he too is being "eaten," not only by the
mutual viciousness of others like Helen (p. 155), but also by what
he considers to be blind fate, as in the case of the torpedo that
destroys his warship before he can kill Nat (p. 186). Indeed,
Pincher's life has been a continuous quarrel with those who
would not comply with his will: "There were the people I got
the better of, people who disliked me, people who quarrelled
with me. Here [on the island] I have nothing to quarrel with. I
am in danger of losing definition" (p. 132).

Most important is Pincher's confrontation with the black
lightning, the cosmic, Godlike force that gradually reduces him
to nothing. An eschatological conflict is presented through Pincher's dialogue and debate with the voice from the darkness. The

image of the black lightning is introduced in chapter 12 (pp. 177–79) and with it comes a dreadful knowledge of Pincher's part. In a recollected conversation with Nathaniel, Pincher remembers his friend's warning about the ultimate extension of human egotism: "Take us as we are now and heaven would be sheer negation. Without form and void. You see? A sort of black lightning, destroying everything that we call life—" (p. 183). This is the afterlife that Pincher has created for himself. Chapter 13 culminates in an extended dialogue between the voice from the darkness and Pincher, who says that he believes only in "the thread of life."

In *Lord of the Flies* and *The Inheritors,* Golding has explored the human potential for evil, and irony has been the novelist's fundamental dramatic device. The supposedly innocent British schoolboys are quick to reveal a terrible capacity for human destruction. The "superior" Homo sapiens in *The Inheritors* is just as prone to murder as to social advancement. And in *Pincher Martin* the stubborn protagonist who defies anything not a part of his own ego must face an eternity of "sheer negation." Rather than epitomizing the indomitable human spirit, Pincher reveals the ultimate evil—total self-absorption, the ego that blindly denies any limitation. Golding has created another variation on a theme that he has developed in the two previous novels—the human capacity for evil and a concomitant blindness to it.

GOLDING USES recurring images of darkness, teeth-mouth, the lobster claw, and excrement to comment on Pincher's depravity. As Louis MacNeice observes, "a study of the symbolism [and imagery] in *Pincher Martin* would show Golding bringing back his thumping motifs as ruthlessly and tellingly as Beethoven."[19] Golding's awareness of the power of images to function as symbols has developed from his own experience in writing poetry.[20] The "vivid poetry of disorder,"[21] which describes the hostile natural elements, gradually shifts to images of either greed or decay, images that define Pincher's own spiritual condition.

The images of blackness are consistent with the idea of Pincher's self-made underworld, and also with the idea of innate fear of the unknown: "the dark represents the truth about him that he has tried to avoid [and] a power beyond him that he will not acknowledge."[22] It is in particular relationship to the image of the dark cellar that all these associations combine. In a letter to John Peter, Golding has explained: "The cellar in *Pincher Martin* represents more than childhood terrors; a whole philosophy in fact—suggesting that God is the thing we turn away from into life, and therefore we hate and fear him and make a darkness there. Yes, very confused but surely legitimately confused because at that depth these aren't ideas as much as feelings. Pincher is running away all the time, always was running, from the moment he had a persona and could say 'I'."[23]

Images referring to blackness are abundant in *Pincher Martin*. The protagonist must survive in the "black choking welter" (p. 7). His beating heart is "the only point of reference in the formless darkness" (p. 10). Everywhere the darkness is "grainless and alike" (p. 13). But apart from the symbolism of chaos and death is the suspicion of an unknown truth: "In the darkness of the skull, it existed, a darker dark, self-evident and indestructible" (p. 45). "Inscrutable darkness [extends] throughout his body" (p. 82). The cellar image, underlining Pincher's fear, is presented at length (pp. 138, 141, 173); Pincher does "anything to fasten the attention away from the interior blackness" (p. 181). All this imagery anticipates the final confrontation with the cosmic force described as the black lightning, the voice from the darkness.

References to devouring teeth and other mouth images constitute a second pattern. Not only do these images emphasize Pincher's voracious appetite and greed (Martin says that eating is the "gross expression of what [is] a universal process"), but also they foreshadow his realization that the island is actually within his own skull, that his jagged rock is indeed a "tooth set in the ancient jaw of a sunken world" (p. 30). His mouth is always working (pp. 17, 46, 80); with a great "snap of teeth" (p. 19) he fights his way toward the limpets. Throughout all his struggles, he recalls his past life, a process of "eating" others, of "crunching up" anyone who got in his way (p. 90). The island is continually compared to his teeth: the rocks break through the muddy earth "as the tooth burst out of the fleshy jaw" (p. 77); he looks "solemnly at the line of rocks and [finds] himself thinking of them as teeth" (p. 78); he names them "the Teeth" (p. 90).

The metaphor of the Chinese maggot box, by which Pincher is compared to a giant maggot that has devoured all the smaller ones (pp. 135–36, 153, 159), again picks up the image of uncontrolled appetite and devouring greed. Pincher's screaming mouth dominates the imagery of chapters 12 and 13, where he is often referred to as simply "the mouth." Ralph Freedman notes that such imagery contributes to the theme: "The verbalizing and rationalizing mouth of reason becomes the sensuous mouth of chaos; domination or control of environment which had regulated his present becomes the compulsive need to dominate which had informed his past; identity achieved through rational control becomes irresponsible domination through the senses by which he is destroyed."[24]

A third pattern, the lobster claw imagery, communicates the grasping, clawing nature of Pincher's ego while also suggesting a wasteland motif, reminiscent of Eliot's Prufrock, who also compares himself to a pair of lobster claws. Pincher's gradual transformation into a pair of giant claws makes a telling comment about the lack of humanity, as he is reduced to an animal level of instinctive behavior. It is particularly ironic that, early in the novel, Pincher himself is repelled by the same images that best describe his own personality: "an ancient antipathy for things with claws set him shuddering" (p. 57). When Pincher later comes upon a lobster, he again is repulsed: "At once, as if his eye had created it, he saw the lobster among the weed, different in dragon-shape, different in colour. He knelt, looking down, mesmerized while the worms of loathing crawled over his skin. 'Beast. Filthy sea-beast'" (p. 112). As chapter 9 opens, Pincher sees two other lobsters before him; when he throws them against the rock, he painfully realizes that they are his own hands (pp. 131–32, 134, 175).

Pincher is rapidly deteriorating into "a great many aches of bruised flesh, a bundle of rags and those lobsters on the rock" (p. 132). His metamorphosis becomes more pronounced: he is turning into a red lobster floating in the sea (p. 167). When he

finally dies again, amid the fury of the black lightning, the transformation is complete: "The centre did not know if it had flung
the body down or if it had turned the world over. There was rock
before its face and it struck with lobster claws that sank in. . . .
Pieces went and there was no more than an island of papery stuff
round the claws and everywhere else there was the mode that
the centre knew as nothing" (p. 201). In the final paragraphs of
chapter 13 nothing remains of Pincher but the claws.

The images pertaining to excrement, as in *Lord of the Flies,*
symbolize humanity's own inner filthiness. On all sides of Pincher's island, seagull dung floats in the dirty water (p. 47). Bird
droppings cover the top portion of the island (p. 58). Pincher
thinks to himself, "I haven't had a crap since we were torpedoed"
(p. 114); he believes that "all the terrors of hell can come down
to nothing more than a stoppage," so his desire to relieve himself
is constantly on his mind (pp. 120, 126, 143). In the background,
the seagulls continue to drop their guano, and the seaweed in
the trenches becomes a stinking cesspool (p. 125). Such imagery
leads to that desperate and also comic scene in which Pincher
gives himself an enema, accompanied by imaginary background
music of Tchaikovsky, Wagner, and Holst. Oldsey and Weintraub
affirm that the "procession of vividly disgusting urinary and fe-
cal metaphors . . . [symbolizes] man's disgusting humanity."[25]
Pincher's last unspoken words, "I shit on your heaven!" (p. 200),
are more pathetic than heroic.

THE NOVEL *Pincher Martin* is a carefully structured moral allegory.
The moment at which Martin recognizes that his predicament is
the result of his distorted egotism, he achieves a self-knowledge
that he has never before attained. Though he is defiant to the end,
he has at least become aware of the consequences of a "religion"
of selfishness: "If his first life has been marked by moral degrada-
tion, his second life reconstitutes the self in moral awareness."[26]
Since Pincher has created God in his own image, he naturally
fears the black lightning, and the inevitable outcome must be his
annihilation.[27]

Golding's novel in no way presupposes a Christian morality
or a conventional theological view. James Gindin contends that

the "rigid schematization in Golding's work tends to force response on the basis of agreement or disagreement with the validity of the author's controlling abstraction." Gindin adds, "Golding's novels are so tightly shaped, so intricately structured, that they rest entirely on the axioms of their Christian visions."[28] Such a belief takes a much too limited view of Golding's work. The hellish landscape of *Pincher Martin* is created by the protagonist himself, and reverses the conventional notion of heaven. Golding considers an eschatological problem without presenting it in "overtly theological terms."[29] The "justice" of Pincher's obliteration by the black lightning is more classically Greek than patently Christian. Bernard Dick has undermined Gindin's thesis with a more accurate estimation of what "happens" in *Pincher Martin*: "The novel is a parody . . . of the Prometheus-Zeus tension, except that in it one finds an antihero and anti-God. Even the most practiced blasphemer never answers the Deity with, 'I shit on your heaven!'; and no Supreme Being, despite his abhorrence of a moral vacuum like Christopher Martin, replies with the annihilation of a soul—a problem that should puzzle even the most liberal theologians."[30] Golding, then, has turned a mythic theme of human endurance into a twentieth-century allegory of humanity's fallen state.

Free Fall 5

In comparison with Golding's first three novels, *Free Fall* appears to be more "social,"[1] more contemporary, more concerned with the existential process of Becoming: "Revelation and recognition of Being, then, gives way to exploration, explanation, discovery of Becoming. . . . So for the first time Golding seems wholly to abandon his isolated and isolating setting and give us the social scene."[2]

However, such an evaluation is misleading. First, though the settings of the earlier novels emphasize isolation, each of these works comments, either directly or indirectly, on the importance of responsible social organization as a counterbalance to individual egotism. Second, the process of Becoming and the moment of self-discovery are closely related, even in the earlier novels. Jack freely chooses to leave Ralph's society, and Ralph eventually realizes what has resulted from such a choice; Tuami is beginning to understand the effects of his people's greedy behavior; even Christopher Martin finally considers his own lost freedom. All these characters have been free to fall. The disintegration of the island society in *Lord of the Flies,* or the flashback technique of *Pincher Martin*, is concerned with the process of Becoming as well as the state of Being.[3]

Even though *Free Fall* emphasizes the search for Becoming much more directly than the other three novels, its major themes are consistent with Golding's earlier work. First, the protagonist's quest for self-knowledge—whether it is undertaken consciously or achieved inadvertently—is crucial to all the novels. Second, the problem of free will versus determinism (central to the process of Becoming) is one of Golding's major preoccupations. Third, Golding again explores the conflict between love (unselfish concern for others) and hate, greed, uncontrolled selfishness. Not only does Sammy Mountjoy, the protagonist of *Free Fall,* learn something about his nature (Being), but also his freedom (Becoming). He chooses to fall, but honest love or unselfishness might have countered such an "inevitability."

Clearly Sammy is more aware of himself and his loss of freedom than any of the characters in Golding's previous fiction. In contrast to Pincher Martin, Sammy "can cry out for help, thereby acknowledging the otherness of the universe and indeed experiencing its divinity."[4] This difference in awareness makes Sammy the most complex and most human of all Golding's characters through the first four novels.

Free Fall presents a different narrative pattern from the previous works. The first person narrative of Sammy Mountjoy places greater emphasis on characterization than the first three novels. Michael Gallagher describes the human image in Golding's first three novels as "clearly one of tragic blackness. We are to be schooled in the awareness of evil and in order to do so, in his grim purgative way, Mr. Golding will admit no contrary pictures to flourish."[5] However, considering the momentary insight of Ralph at the conclusion of *Lord of the Flies,* and Tuami's flicker of self-knowledge in the final chapter of *The Inheritors,* even Gallagher must concede that "with Golding one needs to watch for his final tentative affirmative gestures."[6]

Sammy Mountjoy's level of awareness greatly contributes to the affirmative qualities of *Free Fall.* Beginning with this novel, and culminating in *Darkness Visible,* Golding explores new dimensions of characterization that have little in common with the more conventional patterns of fable, like naive allegory. Neither does Golding's change to a more realistic mode of writing dictate a straightforward reporting of Mountjoy's World War II experiences. Rather, the novel is a collage of impressions, images, and memories—creating, at times, an almost surrealistic effect. Instead of a strict chronological narrative, Sammy's "story" is "an illustration of the incoherence he sets out to explore."[7] *Free Fall* investigates the human reaction to what Golding has called "the patternlessness of life before we impose our patterns on it."[8]

Though the novel begins with a poetic collection of fragmented images, the very first paragraph reveals that Sammy has achieved an insight resulting from the symbolic journey into his own memory. Not only is an allegorical mode suggested by the protagonist's confessed search for self ("When did I lose my freedom?"),[9] but also by elements of timelessness and isolation reminiscent of the earlier novels. Like *Pincher Martin, Free Fall* contains flashback fragments that break down any notion of clock time or chronological arrangement. Sammy selects events and memories in the order in which they are important to him:

> It is a curious story, not so much in the external events which are common enough, but in the way it presents itself to me, the only teller. For time is not to be laid out endlessly like a row of bricks. That straight line from the first hiccup to the last gasp is a dead thing. Time is two modes. The one is an effortless perception native to us as water to the mackerel. The other is a memory, a sense of shuffle fold and coil, of that day nearer than that because more important, of that event mirroring this, or those three set apart, exceptional and out of the straight line altogether. (p. 6)

The subsequent distortion of clock time lends itself to Golding's allegorical purposes. Sammy's recollections resemble little islands of memory, underlining his sense of isolation and separation. His early life in the London slums and his later experiences while recuperating in a children's hospital ward remain timeless and separate: "I was a lifetime in that ward, so that I can switch my mind from the world of Rotten Row to the world of the ward as from planet to planet. I have a sense of timelessness in both places" (p. 70). Sammy refers to his inner self as an "island" (p. 62), reiterating the metaphor that Golding has used so effectively in the earlier novels. Most significantly, Sammy's ordeal in the dark prison cell dramatizes the allegorical implications of the novel: "The process is familiar to the reader of the fables. Left alone on the island of the self, man discovers the reality of his own dark heart."[10]

AS IN THE other novels, Golding uses nomenclature to amplify the symbolism of his story: often proper names in *Free Fall* reveal characterization or theme. The protagonist's name symbolizes the conflict between spiritual vision and crass sensuality, which underlies Sammy's inner torment. He is Samuel, the chosen servant of God (ironically he becomes his *own* judge), and at the same time he is Sammy Mons Veneris, seeking little more than his own physical pleasure.[11] Place names mentioned in the first chapter are expressed with "Bunyanesque bluntness":[12] Sammy's financial success has allowed him to move from Rotten Row, his boyhood slum, to Paradise Hill, whose name mocks Sammy's ever-continuing self-torment. But Rotten Row also represents the innocent world of Sammy's childhood; this "Garden of England" (p. 22) is ironically an Eden to Sammy Mountjoy, the guiltless ragamuffin "wandering in paradise" (p. 45). Evie, the little slum girl whose lies and fantasies kindle Sammy's imagination, is the Eve of this London slum. Even amid the squalor and poverty, Sammy views these early days joyfully: "I crawled and tumbled in the narrow world of Rotten Row, empty as a soap bubble but with a rainbow of colour and excitement round me" (p. 17).

The name of Sammy's naive and rather mindless girl friend, Beatrice Ifor, represents an ironic treatment of Dante, "but the basis of [Sammy's] tragedy is that he confuses, as Dante never did, sharing in [her] Being with possession of the body that manifests it."[13] Not only does "Ifor" equate with "If-or," implying to Sammy that Beatrice can become his long-awaited bridge between the physical and spiritual dualities, but also "I-for [you]," suggesting Sammy's consuming desire to dominate her: "I want you, I want all of you. . . . I want to be with you and in you and on you and round you—I want fusion and identity. . . . Oh God, Beatrice, Beatrice, I love you—I want to be you!" (p. 105). Earlier in the novel Sammy expresses this egotism when he hopes that Beatrice will say, "*I* am *for* you" [italics added]: "if she would only be meeward and if she would be by me and for me and for nothing else" (p. 82). Sammy has gone beyond adoration of the "white body, this body so close to me and unattainable" (p. 104); he desires only to possess, to subjugate, and in so doing he destroys her.

Other character names sustain Golding's irony. Nick Shales's satanic name "belies his personal goodness, but indicates that for Sammy he is nonetheless tempter."[14] Halde, the name given to the sadistic German interrogator who talks easily about "civilization" and "humanity," is often translated as merely "slope," obtusely suggesting the fall motif, the descent from humanity. However, the German word is more precisely a mining term meaning "slag-heap," which evokes a more specific image of degeneration and waste. Most obvious is the name for Father Watts-Watt, the self-deceiving parson who does not know "what's what." Also "watt," associated with light, both mental enlightenment and human warmth, ironically contrasts to the churchman, whose own mental darkness mirrors Sammy's growing confusion: "Everything about him [Father Watts-Watt] was lack-lustre" (p. 224).

A second analogy, which compares a state of nature to a state of mind, is developed in the setting mentioned above. The special beauty that Sammy can see in his environment—the world of Rotten Row—reflects his own innocent state: "We were noisy, screaming, tearful, animal. And yet I remember that time as with the flash and glitter, the warmth of a Christmas party" (p. 17). In addition, the ever-changing kaleidoscope of images and colors that dominate Sammy's mind suggests the patternlessness and mutability of life itself. Sammy's chaotic recollections, revealing his turbulent inner state, are analogous to the formlessness he finds in the world around him, as he translates "incoherence into incoherence" (p. 8). Specifically, his World War II experiences as a prisoner emphasize not only his physical loss of freedom, but also his spiritual loss. The physical blackness of Sammy's prison cell parallels his own inner darkness.

The extrafictional events suggested by the surface narration establish two major biblical motifs: first, Sammy becomes an Adam,[15] who laments his loss of innocence; and second, he is an absurd Christ figure. As Kermode has noted, the combination of the mythic and the moralistic is a major feature of Golding's allegorical technique: "The myth of *Free Fall* is, basically, that of all Golding's books: The Fall of Man, the expulsion from Paradise, erected wit and infected will. . . . Golding's hero is examining his life (made a typical life by many allegorical devices) with a view to discovering a pattern, some connexion between his two worlds of experience [the rational and the spiritual]."[16] Sammy continually stresses that he is not a celebrity, but merely a "burning amateur" (p. 5) searching for a universal truth. At those times when he refers to himself in first person plural, he emphasizes the shared loneliness of all human beings (p. 8). How persons lose their freedom is the subject of his timeless quest.

Sammy projects the absurd saint image as he suffers at the hands of the Nazis. In the interrogation scene, Halde is clearly the tempter: "I have taken you up to a pinnacle of the temple and shown you the whole earth. . . . You have bidden me get behind you" (p. 147). But here again, the scene is a parody of Christ's temptation, for Sammy does "not believe in anything enough to suffer for it or be glad" (p. 144), as Halde correctly observes. Also Sammy is incapable of betraying his fellow soldiers because he simply has no secret military information to reveal. Since Sammy normally chooses to serve his own selfish desires, he would undoubtedly turn traitor if it were possible. On the other hand, his ordeal in the black prison cell does lead to a rethinking of his whole life, and his Lazarus-like resurrection is genuine: "Therefore when the commandant let me out of the darkness he came late and as a second string, giving me the liberty of the camp when perhaps I no longer needed it. I walked between the huts, a man resurrected but not by him" (p. 186).

The plot sequences that manifest the state of Sammy's mind determine the primary structure of the novel. The narrative action is organized through a series of encounters with characters representing polar opposites. These characters, in turn, symbolize the conflicting dualities plaguing Sammy's own conscience. As he looks for a bridge between the psychic-spiritual-mystical realm and the rationalist-physical-empirical world, the emerging conflict is dramatized by the discrepancy between romanticized ideal and disillusioning reality. In each major section of *Free Fall,* Sammy is surrounded by two conflicting characters, one of whom he must reject. In his infants' school days, he idolizes Evie and scorns Minnie, the awkward little girl who urinates in the classroom when she is asked the most rudimentary questions: "We knew that she was not one of us. We were exalted to an eminence. She was an animal down there, and we were all up here" (p. 35). Later, in elementary school, his friendship vacillates between two extremes of personality: the dreamer-adventurer, Johnny Spragg, and the conniver-manipulator, Philip Arnold. At this time in Sammy's life he encounters the quiet perfection of Father Anselm as contrasted to the neurotic weaknesses of Father Watts-Watt. Though Sammy idealizes the luminous Beatrice, he marries the dark, sensual Taffy. While he is drawn to the political idealism of the Communist Party and their speechmaker, Robert Alsopp, he realizes that in actual practice the party membership includes only one worker, Dai Reece, who "never came within a mile of showing any of the textbook reactions. Our army, in fact, was all generals" (p. 96). Finally, a major conflict polarizes in two of Sammy's secondary school teachers, Miss Pringle, the coldhearted religionist, and Mr. Shales, the compassionate science teacher.

To these basic conflicts is added the further irony that the figures representing the spiritual-ideal realm are all considerably flawed characters themselves: Evie is no more than a gutter tramp; Johnny is easily intimidated by school authority; Beatrice is sterile; Alsopp is lecherous and hypocritical; Miss Pringle is unfeeling, bitter, and unable to love. Reconciliation of Sammy's two worlds is impossible, yet his sensitivity to this paradoxical duality is essential to the human condition.

Sammy's decision to possess Beatrice sexually reveals his own new state of mind. When he deliberately chooses to dominate Beatrice, he simultaneously loses his own freedom. In a moment of dramatic irony, he anticipates Beatrice's final surrender, unaware that her physical loss will become his spiritual loss: "suddenly I was overwhelmed by realization that here was the beginning of the end" (p. 109). He soon discovers that "once a human being has lost freedom there is no end to the coils of cruelty" (p. 115). Sammy's rational decision to indulge his own egotism, "though freely taken, makes an end of freedom and brings to his mouth the first taste of evil."[17] Sammy's eventual imprisonment by the Nazis emphasizes what he calls "the dilemma of my spirit" (p. 171). Significantly, his act of looking beyond himself for help occurs at the precise moment of his physical release. His coming out of the dark prison symbolizes his own spiritual rebirth.

SAMMY'S progress toward self-knowledge is underscored by the series of formal questions he asks himself during the course of the interior monologue. As he recollects the major events of his past, he poses the same question on five separate occasions: "Is this the moment I lost my freedom?" And each time the answer is the same: "No. Not here." Whether he is stealing fagcards from smaller boys at his school (p. 52), or whether he is spitting on the church altar, he is merely a pawn manipulated by Philip Arnold (p. 70). The young Samuel of these early days is "innocent of guilt, unconscious of innocence" (p. 78), so Sammy the narrator will have to look elsewhere if he is to discover "the point where this monstrous world of my present consciousness began." He discovers that neither his marriage to Taffy nor his wartime disillusionment has produced that moment of fall (p. 132). Eventually he sees that his initial choice of Shales's rationalism rather than Pringle's spiritualism was not the deciding factor that produced his present state (p. 217). After the ordeal of the prison camp, Sammy is able to identify the moment of his lost freedom: it occurs prior to the war, and it results from his exploitation of Beatrice. Unlike the inadvertent self-discoveries made by Ralph, Tuami, and Pincher, Sammy's revelation is the consequence of his conscious effort to understand what he is.

Recollecting his outer quests for boyhood adventure with Johnny Spragg and Philip Arnold, Sammy seeks "the connection between the little boy, clear as spring water, and the man like a stagnant pool" (p. 9). Only by recounting these surface events can Sammy determine their relation to his inner state. Similarly his prisoner-of-war experiences lead to a drastic change in his spiritual awareness. Also his literal act of searching for Beatrice, after he has returned from the war, reflects his increasing progress toward self-knowledge. He visits her hospital in an attempt to understand, once and for all, his involvement in her lapse into insanity.

Sammy's inner "journey" accounts for the prevailing form of the novel. His elaborate recollections of past experiences and former mental states contribute to the moral allegory of *Free Fall*. Sammy's spiritual pilgrimage is accomplished only after he has addressed the problems of guilt, loss of freedom, and lack of compassion. In the course of this pilgrimage Sammy encounters and rejects rationalist philosophies and political systems: "I have hung all systems on the wall like a row of useless hats. They do not fit. They come from outside, they are suggested patterns" (p. 6). Later he observes "that all patterns have broken one after another, that life is random and evil unpunished" (p. 25). Yet this is not the entire truth about the human condition, and Sammy continues to search.

Sammy's most significant revelation is that he comes to understand the importance of human compassion, a theme only indirectly treated in Golding's earlier novels. During Mountjoy's hospital recovery from a mastoid operation, he experiences a new feeling of elation when he is asked forgiveness by the verger: "Something to forgive is a purer joy than geometry. I've found that out since, as a bit of the natural history of living. It is a positive act of healing, a burst of light" (p. 74). His ordeal in the prison cell leads to the apocalyptic moment when he looks beyond himself for the first time and hopes for deliverance from his nightmare of guilt: "my life has remained centered round the fact of the next few minutes I spent alone and panic-stricken in the dark" (p. 184). His call for help is an act of affirmation. By the end of the novel, Sammy no longer believes that all human beings are either innocent or wicked, but rather that many are simply guilty[18] and must be willing to offer as well as receive love. Such unselfish compassion is a remedy for guilt. "Therefore I have come back . . . to offer forgiveness with both hands" (p. 251), says the new Sammy.

The "battle" motif of this allegorical novel is developed both through Sammy's physical confrontations (his isolation and torture at the hands of the Germans; his sexual conquest of Beatrice) and his philosophical confrontations, with those characters who represent ideologies that he must either accept or reject. The dichotomy established by the two teachers, Mr. Shales and Miss Pringle, demands that Sammy choose either Nick's rationalist, scientific world or the miraculous, spiritual world of his religion teacher.

For a moment, the two worlds exist side by side: "I believe that my child's mind was made up for me as a choice between good and wicked fairies. Miss Pringle vitiated her teaching. She failed to convince, not by what she said but by what she was. Nick persuaded me to his natural scientific universe by what he was, not by what he said" (p. 217). These two teachers are complicated by such ironies of characterization. Sammy chooses Nick for the wrong reason: though there is "no place for spirit" in Nick's scientific method, Sammy is attracted to Shales's love for people and his genuine kindness (p. 213). After later reflection in his adult years, Sammy admits that it is a mistake "to confuse our limitations with the bounds of possibility and clap the universe into a rationalist hat" (p. 9). Miss Pringle, on the other hand, is coldly detached from her pupils, sexually frustrated, and resentful that Father Watts-Watt has turned his attention from her and to Sammy. Her cruelty, prudery, and aloofness turn Sammy against religion, even though he initially is more attracted to spiritualism than to Nick's rationalism. Miss Pringle's unfair accusations that Sammy is drawing obscene pictures during religion class reveals her own inner frustration. She reminds Sammy of Miss Massey, his teacher in elementary school, who had slapped his head three times while proclaiming "God—is—love!" (p. 56). As a result of Sammy's conversations with Shales and Miss Pringle, he recognizes the teachers' influence on his life. The two figures become his "spiritual parents" (p. 194), and in retrospect he sees that they "loom larger behind me as I get older. Mine is the responsibility but they are part reasons for my shape" (p. 214).

As Sammy grows up, he is attracted to the political idealism of the Communist Party, and his debate with Philip Arnold about the values of communism marks another philosophical confrontation. The sarcastic Philip sees what Sammy would like to ignore: Alsopp's lecherous interest in the young women of his organization; the absurdity of having only one token "worker," Dai Reece, who "wants booze more than anything" (p. 99); Sammy's own desperation in latching onto a ready-made "system." Unable to counter Philip's criticism, Sammy withdraws uneasily, "feeling my own uncertainties, my lopsided and illogical life" (p. 100). Sammy's dialogue with the headmaster at his school and also his confrontation with Dr. Enticott reveal additional truths about Sammy's moral condition. Though the advice is lost on young Sammy at the time, the headmaster, after calling the boy "dishonest and selfish," adds one final but important word: "I'll tell you something which may be of value. I believe it to be true and powerful—therefore dangerous. If you want something enough, you can always get it provided you are willing to make the appropriate sacrifice. Something, anything. But what you get is never quite what you thought; and sooner or later the sacrifice is always regretted" (p. 235).

Ironically Sammy uses similar language when later seducing Beatrice: "I would take any consequences that ensued would I not, who was so breathlessly assuring her that there would be no consequences" (p. 117). Because Sammy at this time is incapable of loving Beatrice in any way other than through sexual intercourse, he assumes, in effect, that his act of physical domination has no moral consequences or responsibilities. When he finally faces Beatrice in the hospital where she is confined as a mental patient, he understands the nature of his guilt. He recognizes the harmful results of his "experiment" (p. 237) in egotism. Dr. Enticott's indictment of Sammy is similar to Pete's condemnation of Pincher Martin: it is a matter of selfishness. When Sammy asks that Beatrice's case be kept secret, for fear that it would endanger his career, Enticott declares, "You and your bloody pictures. You use everyone. You used that woman [Beatrice]. You used Taffy. And now you've used me" (p. 246).

The novel has come full circle in this scene. The asylum is located in the general's home, the same building that Sammy and Johnny Spragg had explored in their childhood days. Like the helpless Minnie of Sammy's early memories, Beatrice urinates on the hospital floor. The once beautiful Beatrice is little more than a pathetic, mindless animal. Sammy understands that he, more than any other factor, is responsible for her condition. This is the terrible knowledge from which he has been running. In addition to the rationalist world of "cause and effect, the law of succession, statistical probability," Sammy acknowledges "the moral order, sin and remorse. . . . Both worlds exist side by side. They meet in me" (p. 244).

In Dr. Halde, Sammy is confronted with the personification of pure reason. Halde is a striking contrast to Nick Shales; the German psychologist possesses no warmth, no human emotion, no compassion. Though Halde speaks English more precisely than Sammy, the doctor's voice is inhumanly cold: "his was the foreign voice, nationless, voice of the divorced idea, a voice that might be conveyed better by the symbols of mathematics than printed words" (p. 135). He says that his harsh interrogation tactics are used only "for the sake of humanity" (p. 142), and that he is dedicated to "a higher truth" (p. 143). When his prisoner does not capitulate, Halde quickly has Sammy placed in solitary confinement in a small, pitch-black cell. Although Halde does not recognize the human, spiritual dimension, he is ironically accurate in his analysis of Sammy:

> There is no point at which something has knocked on your door and taken possession of you. You possess yourself. Intellectual ideas, even the idea of loyalty to your country sits on you loosely. You wait in a dusty waiting-room on no particular line for no particular train. And between the poles of belief, I mean the belief in material things and the belief in a world made and supported by a supreme being, you oscillate jerkily from day to day, from hour to hour. Only the things you cannot avoid, the sear of sex or pain, avoidance of the one suffering repetition and prolongation of the other, this constitutes what your daily consciousness would not admit, but experiences as life. Oh, yes, you are capable of a certain degree of love, but nothing to mark you out from the ants or the sparrows. (pp. 144–45)

Halde's own inhumanity results from his limited view; he sees only with the scientist's eye. Though Halde "knows a tremendous amount about 'peoples,' especially Sammy, . . . he cannot foresee the spiritual illumination granted the fallen man."[19] However, Sammy's realization that his own guilt separates him from both innocence *and* evil is not a settling conclusion. The commandant's final words—"The Herr Doctor does not know about peoples"—are an inscrutable puzzle to Sammy, for the doctor all too well has recognized humanity in its absurdity. But for Sammy there is the hope of something more: if guilt is an inevitable condition of modern life, human compassion becomes all the more essential.

SAMMY USES the image of life-as-a-painting to communicate his quest for meaning. The other dominant images in *Free Fall*—blackness, excrement, falling—emphasize the theme of human guilt and spiritual corruption.

By comparing life with painting, Sammy hopes to reconstruct a picture of his own life. He calls his vivid reminiscences "the backward sight which hangs events in their symbolic colours" (p. 28). Such imagery contributes to the quest motif. Sammy's recollections will organize life just as the rectangular borders of a canvas order the subjects of a painting: "The mind cannot hold more than so much; but understanding requires a sweep that takes in the whole of remembered time and then can pause. Perhaps if I write my story as it appears to me, I shall be able to go back and select. Living is like nothing because it is everything—is too subtle and copious for unassisted thought. Painting is like a single attitude, a selected thing" (p. 7).

Sammy attempts to "catch the picture before the perception vanishes" (p. 15). The effect is similar to freeze-framing a portion of moving film, as when he describes his mother in Rotten Row (p. 15). He does not hesitate, however, to adjust his image in order to capture essence: "I can remember her only in clay, the common earth, the ground; I cannot stick the slick commercial colours on stretched canvas for her or outline her in words that are ten thousand years younger than her darkness and warmth"

(p. 16). Because of Sammy's "good and trained colour sense" (p. 17), he can describe an April day with the striking imagery of a painter of words: "What other month could give me such blue and white, such sun and wind? The clothing on the lines was horizontal and shuddering, the sharp, carved clouds hurried, the sun spattered from the soap suds in the gutter, the worn bricks were bright with a dashing of rain. It was the sort of wind that gives grown-ups headaches and children frantic exultation" (p. 20). The description is as vivid as an imagist poem. The red brick glistening after a rain recalls the central image in William Carlos Williams's "The Red Wheelbarrow."

Since Golding's narrator is a painter, *Free Fall* experiments even more freely with the power of images than the three earlier novels did. Sammy's feelings "are represented by colours" (p. 70), as he externalizes his innermost thoughts. His impressions of the children's ward, at the beginning of chapter 3, are presented through a kaleidoscopic series of color images. When Sammy ends the chapter by recalling his innocent childhood days, his metaphor again turns to painting and color: "Let me think in pictures again. If I imagine heaven metaphorically dazzled into colours, the pure white light spread out in a cascade richer than a peacock's tail then I see one of the colours lay over me. I was innocent of guilt, unconscious of innocence; happy, therefore, and unconscious of happiness. Perhaps the full sheaf of colours is never to be experienced by the human being since if he experiences these colours they must lie in the past or on someone else" (pp. 77–78).

In a similar manner Sammy describes the new traffic lights in the South London slum district: "They were so new a thing in those days that an art student like myself could not see them without thinking of ink and wash—ink line for the sudden punchball shape, wash for the smokes and glows and the spilt suds of autumn in the sky" (p. 79).

Sammy often thinks about Beatrice from the perspective of a painter: her grey suit with alternating stripes of green and white; a gold chain dangling around her glossy white throat; the blush of pink on her cheeks when Sammy asks her personal questions. Whether he is designing Christmas cards for her (p.

225) or losing himself in the lush greeness of the forest near the town (p. 235), his thoughts are obsessed by the image of her white body. It is through such vivid images that he selects the "pictures" of his past, as he concretizes experience in a desperate quest to understand himself.

Images of blackness and darkness, recurrent in all Golding's novels, symbolize the dark, irrational, self-destructive forces within oneself. Human nature tries "to impose a pattern on the world, to escape at all cost from the cloacal darkness of an original void to which [it] is forced back by an irrational life force."[20] In the prison cell Sammy confronts beasts of his own making, just as the boys of *Lord of the Flies,* the Homo sapiens, and Pincher Martin have all externalized their own guilty fear of "things that scuttle or slide or crawl" (p. 177). Sammy's "dark cell becomes a chamber of horrors, created *ex nihilo* by the perverse imagination of a fallen man."[21] Death and life are twisted into a monstrous nightmare vision as Sammy reverts to the womb and simultaneously faces the extinction of death. Though he is only in a broom closet with a damp mop in the center of the floor, Sammy imagines the worst, just as Halde knew he would. The "unnameable, unfathomable and invisible darkness that sits at the centre" of Sammy's being (p. 8) is the result of his inner guilt and spiritual isolation. Sammy is susceptible to the most primitive fears. When he touches the wet mop in the dark, his hand instinctively recoils, "a hand highly trained by the tragedies of a million years" (p. 179). His torture is self-inflicted; only his plea for help shatters the darkness.

As in *Lord of the Flies* and *Pincher Martin,* images pertaining to excrement and filth underline the theme of human, spiritual depravity. The world of Rotten Row is a world of dirt and lavatories (p. 19), a world where Evie urinates standing up (p. 31), and where Minnie relieves herself right in the schoolroom (p. 35). The image recurs during Sammy's last view of the once beloved Beatrice, as she urinates on the hospital floor. In tracing his own progress from the clear stream of his youth to the "stagnant pool" of his adulthood, Sammy records his squalid prison life. Confined to a black cell of imaginary horrors, Sammy projects his own sexual guilt by imagining that the Germans have cut off the penis of a decaying dead body that shares Sammy's fetid prison (p. 182). As a result of his ordeal in the darkness, Sammy frantically objectifies his own diseased spirit.

Consistent with the fall-of-humankind motif are the images of falling that dominate the novel. One of Sammy's most vivid childhood memories is that of watching, with Johnny Spragg, a small aircraft crash to earth in a fiery holocaust (p. 41). Earlier the boys had speculated about such a calamity, and now the prospect becomes a terrible reality. Like the crash of the capsule or like the fall of the parachutist in *Lord of the Flies,* the literal act takes on symbolic overtones. At crucial times throughout Sammy's life, he expresses his sensation of falling. Often it is a literal experience, as when he falls to the floor of the church after being knocked off his feet (p. 62), or when he is dumped onto the concrete floor of his prison cell (p. 153); sometimes it is a figurative fall, as when Sammy speculates about the inability of his Communist Party to avert the coming war: "The world around us was sliding on and down through an arch into a stormy welter where morals and families and private obligations had no place" (p. 95).

An additional image of falling is contained in the title of the novel itself. The title *Free Fall* possesses both theological implications concerning Adam's fall, and also scientific implications referring to twentieth-century humanity's suspension in space, beyond gravitational controls. Golding says that the title "is in fact a scientific term. It is where your gravity has *gone*; it is a man in a space ship who has no gravity; things don't fall or lift, they float about. . . . Where for hundreds of thousands of years men have known where they were, now they don't know where they are any longer. This is the point of *Free Fall*."[22] Inasmuch as one major pattern of conflict in *Free Fall* concerns the opposing worlds of theology and science, the title is all the more appropriate.

THE NARRATIVE action of *Free Fall* accommodates four "levels" of meaning. First, the novel contains a moral allegory that explores the nature of free will and the consequences of unethical behavior. Sammy searches for the moment at which he lost his freedom, and eventually discovers the awful responsibility that he must take for Beatrice's condition. Second, Sammy's interior monologue dramatizes the psychological conflicts that torment the psyche of modern humanity—the opposing worlds of rationality and spirituality that can never be bridged. Third, the narrative pattern of the novel incorporates a system of archetypal motifs that enlarge the significance of Sammy's struggle. The archetypal patterns of journey, initiation, and quest represent civilization's universal attempt to understand itself. Sammy's progress from ignorance to insight is complemented symbolically by his movement from darkness to light. Finally, the novel implies that part of Sammy's condition is a result of the war and the twentieth-century social environment. In this respect the allegory communicates the deterioration of society and the resultant alienation of modern humanity after World War II. There is a close connection between Sammy's inner chaos and the war-torn world in which he lives: "I welcomed the destruction that war entails, the deaths and terror. Let the world fall. There was anarchy in the mind where I lived and anarchy in the world at large, two states so similar that the one might have produced the other" (pp. 131–32).

Though Sammy concludes his autobiography with the idea that "there is no bridge" (p. 253) between the rational and spiritual worlds, between the past and the present, between selfishness and sacrifice, Golding has, in effect, created such a bridge. Sammy's very act of questioning is a positive gesture.[23] His search for self has ended in disillusionment and uncertainty, but Sammy is a wiser man. He understands, more than any of the characters in the earlier Golding novels, that to be human is to be guilty; but more significantly, he discovers the importance of human compassion. Thus he proclaims that he will come back to "live in two worlds at once—to offer forgiveness with both hands" (p. 251). Sammy will not be defeated by the knowledge of his own imperfections; rather, he will take consolation in the reconstructive power of unselfish good will toward his fellow human beings: "a kind of vital morality, not the relationship of a man to remote posterity nor even to a social system, but the relationship of individual to individual man—once an irrelevance but now seen to be the forge in which all change, all value, all life is beaten out into a good or a bad shape" (p. 189).

The Spire 6

The Spire demonstrates Golding's skill at transforming what appear to be simple narrative materials into a subtle, complicated drama of human conflict. The central symbol of the novel at first seems overly obvious: a four-hundred-foot church tower constructed upon a weak, corrupt foundation; presumably this spire represents the monolithic viewpoint of its obsessed creator, Dean Jocelin. But Golding's novel is not so predictable. Instead, it explores the paradoxical interrelationships between good and evil, the ambiguity of society's moral systems, and the self-delusions of a totally unreliable narrator. The spire symbolizes not only pride and blinding egotism but also vitality and creativity. This one symbol epitomizes the tragic nature of the human condition. The story of Jocelin's building the tower is a study in both the construction and destruction of his human resources.

The technique of *The Spire,* as in Golding's other novels, depends heavily on irony; on intense, poetic language; on the manipulation of point of view. Also Golding's major themes—self-discovery, free will versus determinism, love versus selfishness—all recur in *The Spire.*

Contributing to the illusion of simplicity, the narrative pattern is straightforward, with none of the flashback techniques like those in *Pincher Martin* or *Free Fall* to obscure the action. However, clock time in the novel is deemphasized. Similar to the isolated locales of Golding's earlier fiction, the setting in fourteenth-century England, during the construction of the great cathedrals, sufficiently circumscribes the narration, an isolation conducive to the timeless world of allegory. There is little mention of the passage of days and nights: "time is not reckoned with precision because Jocelin measures it only in terms of progress or delay in construction of the spire."[1] On those occasions when Jocelin meditates about the progress of his cathedral spire, all time stops: "He passed, in this frozen attitude, through a point of no time and no sight."[2] The sequence of "mental events," through which he comes to understand his own destructive nature, does not follow any set chronology. In this timeless setting, Jocelin's actions take on allegorical significance. As he comes nearer to completing the construction of the spire, he ironically comes closer to the demoralizing truth about himself. Stressing the importance of a solid foundation on which to work, the wife of the master builder for Jocelin's spire cites the architectural principle that a spire should go down as far as it goes up (p. 39). Such a statement describes Jocelin's symbolic progress toward self-discovery. He will have to look beneath the lip service to divine inspiration, in order to understand what the spire really means for his own life.

The impetus for Golding's previous fiction came from literary sources, such as his ironic treatment of Ballantyne, Wells, Defoe, and Dante. No such stimulus, however, affected the writing of *The Spire*. Though the story is reminiscent of Ibsen's *The Master Builder* (1892) and also *Brand* (1866),[3] Golding does not mention Ibsen when discussing the sources for his novel. He comments that his interest in cathedrals emerged from living in Salisbury for many years. He denies any attempt to "turn Trollope upside down," though the original title for the novel was *Barchester Spire:* "I was in an ideal situation to write my book about Barchester, and it didn't really turn out to be a Barchester novel at all."[4] Golding further adds that he by no means wanted the book to be "medieval" or "historical," but rather something larger and less restricted to a particular time and place.[5]

The connection between Jocelin and the spire is so close that one figure becomes a function of the other. There is purposely "a diminished sense of the actuality of the novel's physical world; the construction of the spire is often treated in meticulous detail, but the men who build it are dim shadows, performing dim actions in undefined space,"[6] for this is the realm of allegory. Jocelin's symbolic journey toward self-knowledge is the central subject of the novel. His obsessive "vision" of the rising spire results in physical calamities for his associates and spiritual blindness for himself; consequently, Jocelin's gradual awareness of his tragic condition is presented through a complex moral allegory.

THE PROPER names in *The Spire* are particularly appropriate to the characters they identify. "Jocelin," more than recalling the name of two other thirteenth-century churchmen (Jocelin de Brakelond, noted for his "forthright, familiar, clear and convincing" narratives of medieval church life;[7] and Jocelin of Wells, who rebuilt much of the cathedral at St. John's[8]), also literally means "jest," "trifle," "joke." Though Jocelin is undaunted when the townspeople call the spire "Jocelin's Folly," his own moral blindness makes the project as much a mockery of misplaced egotism as it is the honor to God that Jocelin professes it to be. It is particularly appropriate that Jocelin's name recalls both the associations with medieval church life and also the ironies connected with the Latin *jocus.* The reader soon discovers that Jocelin's life is simultaneously joy and joke.[9]

In the manner of a Hawthorne story, other character names suggest the more abstract dimensions of the narrative. Pangall, the impotent, lame custodian of the cathedral, endures a life of "pain" and "gall," as each day he is bitterly humiliated by the construction workers, who joke about his masculinity. The secret love affair carried on by his beautiful wife, Goody, affords an ironic comment on her name (reminiscent of "Faith," the name for the wife in Hawthorne's "Young Goodman Brown"). Since Roger Mason and his wife Rachel are so closely linked together, their names begin with the same letter: "Not only were they inseparable, but alike in appearance; more like brother and sister than man and wife, dark, sturdy, red-lipped. They were islanded, and their life was a pattern of its own" (p. 39).

Father Adam's name connotes an archetypal universality appropriate to Jocelin's final dying vision. Looking into Father Adam's face, Jocelin sees the frailty and corruption of all humanity—the vision of the fallen Adam that so dominates Golding's fiction:

> Then his mind trotted away again and he saw what an extraordinary creature Father Adam was, covered in parchment from head to foot, parchment stretched or tucked in, with curious hairs on top and a mad structure of bones to keep it apart. Immediately, as in a dream that came between him and the face, he saw all people naked, creatures of light brown parchment, which bound in their pipes or struts. He saw them pace or prance in sheets of woven stuff, with the skins of dead animals under their feet and he began to struggle and gasp to leave this vision behind him in words that never reached the air. *How proud their hope of hell is. There is no innocent work.* (p. 214)

The relationships between a state of nature and a state of mind occur in three recognizable patterns. First, the discovery that the church itself is constructed upon swampland emphasizes the parallel between the physical foundations tottering in the black, watery mire and the church fathers' (specifically Jocelin's) own spiritual hypocrisy: "At one point the waters burst through the floor, as if mother earth—nature arrayed against spirit—were intent on punishing the presumption of the builders."[10] Furthermore, the pillars of the cathedral at times rumble in the shaky earth, drowning out the choir and creating an ominous note of disaster. The vibrating pillars foreshadow the destructive results of Jocelin's obsession; they also signal the gradual disintegration of his initial idealism, though he does not readily admit there is any danger. The exterior circumstances of the rumbling stones reflect the fearful inner turmoil of both the townspeople and Jocelin himself. The atmosphere is highly charged with dread and anticipation:

> Late in December the stones began to sing again. They did not sing all the time; and in the Lady Chapel there were whole weeks together when the choir could sing unhindered. But then men would be aware of some vague discomfort, and, trying to define it, would decide that the air was too dry or too cold; only to find at last that there was a needle in each ear, and that breath had a tendency to hold itself for no reason whatever. Then the needles would become audible, so that breath let itself out in long expiration, to be replaced by exasperation and fear. (p. 108)

Though Jocelin tells his followers, "It will pass," his words are hollow and unconvincing. The rumbling earth continues to shake both the spire and Jocelin's faith in himself: "As winter moved towards spring, and the crocuses towards the surface of the earth, and the tower towards the sky, the stones sang more frequently" (p. 109).

Second, Jocelin's physical condition—his spine eaten away by tuberculosis—is but an outward manifestation of his own spiritual disease. Jocelin's condition is not so much an organic malady as it is a psychological ailment: "It was his back which had given way as he tried to destroy the pillars and seemingly it is of this disease he dies. Yet, on his deathbed he hears a significant argument as to whether he is dying of consumption of the spine or from heart trouble. By then his sufferings in heart at the realization of his own cruelty are more than the pains in his back."[11] This symbolism is extended when the spire itself is compared to a man lying on his back. Spire and spine are mixed together in an important, recurring metaphor. Early in the novel Jocelin compares the model of the cathedral to "a man lying on his back. The nave was his legs placed together, the transepts on either side were his arms outspread. The choir was his body; and the Lady Chapel, where now the services would be held, was his head. And now also, springing, projecting, bursting, erupting from the heart of the building, there was its crown and majesty, the new spire" (p. 4).

To increase the identification with his own body, Jocelin later dreams that he himself is lying on his back in the wet marshland, his arms like the transepts of the cathedral (p. 59). In his diary, Jocelin writes that he had visualized the whole building as a human image (p. 185). In a moment of dramatic irony, and *before* he realizes that the spire is as shaky as his own frail spine, he writes that his "heart seemed to be building the church in me, walls, pinnacles, sloping roof, with a complete naturalness and inevitability of consent" (p. 186). What Jocelin imagines to be a "guardian angel" deep within him, "like the warmth of a fire at his back, powerful and gentle at the same time; and so immediate was the pressure of that personality, it might have been in his very spine" (pp. 17–18), is really the gnawing tuberculosis. Even after the disease renders him crippled and helpless, one of his last living moments is spent in the realization that he is "like a building about to fall" (p. 214). Jocelin's physical illness becomes a metaphor for his spiritual decay, and both states are symbolized in the tottering spire, the unifying image of the novel.

A third pattern by which a natural, physical condition reflects an inner mental state is represented in the character of the dumb man, whom Howard Babb has called the most "purely symbolic" in the novel: the speechless man "is associated in various ways with the physical self that Jocelin keeps straining to repress."[12] Jocelin represses not only his sexual desires but more importantly the knowledge of his own destructive egotism. For Jocelin, knowledge of this monstrous self remains subliminal throughout much of the novel, and he is no more able to articulate his true feelings than the mute man is able to talk.

Two extrafictional dimensions expand the surface action of the novel: (1) Jocelin as Christ figure (the absurd saint motif); (2) the parody of the Abraham-Isaac story. Jocelin's struggles are compared, for purposes of irony, to the passion of Christ. In his dream, Jocelin imagines himself crucified, while the townspeople jeer at him (p. 59). The image of crucifixion is sustained with descriptions of Jocelin "impaled on his will" (p. 109), the victim of his own selfish obsessions rather than a martyr to his religious vision. When he battles the raging winds that threaten to topple the spire, his struggles recall Christ's suffering: "A handful of something struck his face and left a stinging behind as if it had been nettles. He fell in the lee of a hummock with a wooden cross on it and the skirt of his gown flogged him, so he pulled it up through his belt. A lath came from somewhere and raised a cruel welt on his thigh" (p. 168). Jocelin even uses parables (pp. 111–12 and 117) to dignify his monomaniacal plans. He is the saint who cannot find forgiveness for himself, as his last meeting with Roger Mason reveals. As he leaves Mason's house, he also is met with "a sea of imprecation and hate" from the jeering townspeople (p. 207). He has seen his angel ironically turn to devil; more evil than good has come from the construction of the spire.

On the opening page of the novel, as Jocelin rejoices in the sunlight shining through the stained glass picture of Abraham and Isaac, he imagines that his own dedication to God (and to the building of the spire) is as pure and unquestioning as Abraham's. But Jocelin does not hesitate to sacrifice anyone to the construction of his tower; his unfeeling, unthinking will stops at nothing. Before he is finished, he will have sacrificed Pangall, Goody, Roger and Rachel Mason, as well as himself: "The story of Abraham and Isaac is more than a picture now. But the sacrifice which in fact follows [Pangall's death as well as Roger Mason's bitter disillusionment] is a terrible parody of the story of the man of faith."[13] Jocelin's dedication to God becomes merely blind willfulness.

The major analogy of *The Spire* involves the relationship between building the tower and Jocelin's growing egotism—the relationship between physical act and state of mind. Just as the spire threatens to fall, so Jocelin's monomania threatens to destroy all those who succumb to his domination. Father Adam's offhand comment that "life itself is a rickety building" (p. 183) expresses the predominant metaphor of the novel. When Jocelin extends his control over the workers and by a sheer "act of will" pushes the tower higher and higher, he also risks the tragic outcome of his overreaching pride. Though he is convinced that he is remaining humble, the interior narrative reveals a different Jocelin: "He felt if he were given the chance he could hold up the whole building on his own shoulders" (p. 69). "He thought at first timidly, then proudly, then timidly again, in an infinite regression, . . . [that] he had done well in forcing the tower up against all opposition" (p. 70). Jocelin plays the role of God (just as egotisti-cally as Pincher Martin) when he assumes that his will "is linked to a Will without limit or end" (p. 79). Such a conviction allows him to coerce Roger Mason into continuing the construction past the point of safety. Not only does Jocelin ensure that Goody will be nearby (the dean knows of her affair with Roger), but he also takes the liberty to cancel Roger's other work at Malmesbury. Jocelin thinks of himself as married to the spire (p. 88), and as-sumes that by his own domineering will (pp. 35 and 89) he can thrust the master builder up and up, until the tower reaches four hundred feet: "and now my will has to support a whole world up there" (p. 91).

The theme of uncontrolled egotism is recurrent in Golding's novels. Jack's ability to dominate the hunters; the difference be-tween Homo sapiens and the simple Neanderthals; Pincher Mar-tin's refusal to die; Sammy Mountjoy's exploitation of Beatrice—all of this has developed from the same tragic predicament, the novelist is saying. In humanity's attempt to transcend itself, it stumbles into the dark cellarage of selfishness, pride, and the ex-ploitation of other human beings.

THE PROGRESS of the protagonist toward self-knowledge and to-ward increased human feeling is presented through two interre-lated motifs. First, the outer, physical quest to build the spire pro-vides the major setting for symbolic action. As the tower slowly rises, there emerges a second motif of progress—Jocelin's spiri-tual journey toward understanding and compassion. In a moment of dramatic irony, before Jocelin fully comprehends the awful significance of his actions, his naive remarks imply an unfolding moral allegory: "I never guessed in my folly that there would be a new lesson at every level" (p. 103). But Golding's allegory is considerably more complicated than are Jocelin's pat homilies. The novel is saved from obviousness and predictability because the "lessons" that Jocelin eventually learns are not those to which he so glibly alludes during the first part of the narrative. For Jocelin, apocalypse will be accompanied by paradox and am-biguity.

A major theme presented in the surface action of the novel

is that of cost, the human cost of a spiritual vision distorted by the sordidness of the real world. Thus the outer quest to construct the spire is attended by physical perils from the raging elements, defections from within the ranks of the workers, and even a ritual murder.

Not since *Lord of the Flies* has a Golding novel followed such a balanced structure. As each stage of the spire is completed, the cost in human resources increases. In the beginning, the rumbling foundations and the whistling winds threaten the workers' progress. Ranulf, the most serious and professional of the workers, simply leaves without saying a word. As the tower grows, Jocelin and even the master builder suffer paralyzing spells of vertigo. When the construction reaches three hundred fifty feet, Jehan, another worker whom Jocelin trusts, proclaims that the pillars are bending and that the building project is doomed. The superstitious workers, who have already killed one man in a frenzy of human sacrifice (p. 10), vent their fears on the helpless Pangall, much as the terrified boys of *Lord of the Flies* destroy Simon. Eventually Goody dies painfully in the act of childbirth, after being antagonized by Rachel Mason, who is suffering with the knowledge of her husband's infidelity. By the time the tower is complete, Roger is left a broken and disillusioned man, a victim of Jocelin's willful manipulations.

During the course of these mounting calamities, Jocelin begins to change. His inner, spiritual progress—his developing moral awareness that is gradually unfolding to the reader—becomes the focus of the novel. Before the spire is completed, Roger Mason, who sees the destructiveness of Jocelin's vision, asks, "And can't you see what you've done?" Jocelin merely laughs with joyous excitement, "I know! I know! Indeed I know!" (p. 98). But he does not know. When he guardedly admits to himself that the marriage he had arranged between Goody and Pangall must inevitably end in human misery for both, he simply dismisses the problem as "the cost of building material" (p. 121). As Jocelin considers his situation more carefully, he finds it increasingly difficult to ignore the cost: "But what with the dead woman, the present impossibility of prayer, and the defection of a workman,

Jocelin could only put his hands to his ears and rock himself"
(p. 136). When he discovers the twig of mistletoe used in the
workmen's pagan rituals, he senses what has happened to
Pangall. His conscience torments him, as his heavenly vision
turns to hellish nightmare: "the replaced paving stones were hot
to his feet with all the fires of hell" (p. 151). Evil ironically
emerges from the "good"; the sacred becomes the profane; and
Jocelin is bewildered by the paradox: "It's another lesson. The
lesson for this height. Who could have foreseen that this was part
of the scheme? Who could know what at this height the thing I
thought of as a stone diagram of prayer would lift up a cross and
fight eye to eye with the fires of the devil?" (p. 150).

Jocelin's inner revelations about himself and those around
him contribute to the pattern of spiritual pilgrimage, much more
than does his outer attempt to crown the spire with the Holy Nail.
During the course of the novel, Jocelin discovers that he is the
victim of his own monstrous selfishness; that he can no longer
ignore the inhumanity of his tactics in building the spire (he is
no less guilty for his own offenses than are the pagan workmen
who directly murder Pangall); that he is often motivated not by
religious fervor but by a repressed sexuality; that meaningful
communication between human beings is a difficult and seldom
realized accomplishment; that the people around him are at
heart ineffectual and hypocritical (particularly his fellow churchmen). Though several critics have used differing terms to classify
the "stages" of the protagonist's spiritual progress, the allegorical
method by which Jocelin gains the bitter knowledge about himself unmistakably involves the battle motif.

The confrontations with the "angels" of good and evil, Lady
Alison, Father Anselm, and Roger Mason finally reveal to Jocelin
his self-deception and moral blindness.

Jocelin's self-doubts are symbolized by the conflict between
his imaginary good angel (pp. 45 and 59) and the antagonistic
force he associates with the devil (pp. 70 and 91). As his obsession with the spire grows stronger, he is unable to distinguish
between the good or the evil angel: "The confusion was in his
head again. He said dizzily to himself: It's the cost! What else

should I have expected?" (p. 100). At this point he can no longer pray for Pangall, Goody, or any of his congregation: "I can't pray for them since my whole life has become one prayer of will." The warmth he feels at the back of his spine and that he first identifies with the good angel becomes a painful, hellish fire—the spreading tuberculosis that eventually kills him. When he climbs down the construction ladders "with his angel," Roger Mason whispers, "I believe you're the devil. The devil himself" (p. 118). Angel and devil visit Jocelin regularly (p. 124). When he looks at the spire, the halo-like glow from the workers' fires in the tower changes to infernal "streams of sparks" (p. 125). The physical disease in his spine and the spiritual infirmities of his heart continue to torment him. His life becomes a confusion of pain and passion: "Often, his angel stood at his back; and this exhausted him, for the angel was a great weight of glory to bear, and bent his spine. Moreover, after a visit by the angel—as if to keep him in his humility—Satan was given leave to torment him, seizing him by the loins, so that it became indeed an unruly member" (p. 133).

When Jocelin sees his image reflected in a piece of sheet metal used at the construction site, he believes he is being confronted by the devil himself: "For a moment he thought of exorcism, but when he lifted his hand, the figure raised one too" (p. 149). As he becomes more neurotic, he declares, "I know what it is. It's become a race between me and the devil" (p. 154). His troubled mind is the battlefield on which angel and devil fight for supremacy (p. 165). He eventually cannot discriminate between devil, townspeople, himself, or even the red-haired Goody; his hellish dreams reveal his tormented spirit and his sexual guilt. His sense of persecution intensifies: "The devils still had possession of the nave though the spire was safe from them. But he was not safe from them himself. His angel left him, and the sweetness of his devil was laid on him like a hot hand" (p. 170).

When Jocelin finally discovers that the church pillars are filled only with rubble and that his life's work is built on nothing more substantial, his "angel" crushes his spine with a burning, paralytic stroke. Jocelin's remaining lucid moments occur only

when all angels leave him so that he can think (p. 182). As with
the other confrontations in the novel, Jocelin moves from ignorance to insight. The way angel and devil merge as one ambiguous figure is consistent with the paradox of the spire itself.

Jocelin's meeting with his aunt, Lady Alison, who is also mis-
tress to the king, forces him to reexamine his own position in
the church hierarchy. He has assumed that he was chosen for his
holy occupation by God. Such a belief makes it easier for Jocelin
to rationalize his exploitation of others: all who work on the spire
are simply the instruments of a divine plan. Lady Alison, however,
tells Jocelin the truth. She merely used her sexual charms to secure a favor from the king. Partly as a spite to her dull sister and
partly as a whim, she chose the dreariest occupation she could
imagine for her young nephew. After years have passed, Jocelin
is now shocked to hear Lady Alison's flippant confession. She
even tells him that she is intimate with Bishop Walter of Rome.
As a result of his confrontation with Lady Alison, Jocelin is per-
plexed by the way the sacred and the sensual have become entangled, by the knowledge that his appointment as dean has been
determined by the random whimsies of his harlot aunt, and by
the haunting realization that his own repressed sexual longings
for Goody have been the unacknowledged motivation for his behavior. When Lady Alison sees her nephew's bitter disillusionment, she comforts him by saying that he must continue to believe in his vocation (p. 179). At this point, the roles are ironically
reversed: the whore becomes the confessor, and the churchman
admits his adulterous passions.

The confrontation with Father Anselm reveals to Jocelin that
for years his fellow churchman has hidden feelings of resentment. Though Anselm is correct in condemning the way Jocelin
has willfully manipulated others at the expense of the church, his
rebukes are motivated more by jealousy than by moral indignation. Nevertheless, Anselm's bitter pronouncements leave Jocelin
speechless. It is true that Jocelin has seen nothing and understood nothing for years (p. 193), that his confessions have been
more self-congratulatory than contrite, and that he has dispensed
with church services for the sake of the spire. When an aston-

ished Jocelin asks Anselm what kind of priest he is, the answer is blunt: "You should know. The same sort as you, if you like. Minimal" (p. 194).

Jocelin is moved by his colleague's harshness, even though he recognizes that pride and greed are parts of Anselm's motivation (Anselm derives his income from the sale of candles for the church services, but Jocelin has canceled further ceremonies). Anselm rebukes Jocelin for trying to "make a man of my years and standing into a builder's mate" (p. 195). Jocelin ignores the personal pettiness of his accuser, and takes the criticism seriously. The dean regrets being so blind to the feelings of those around him. When he asks Father Anselm's forgiveness, it is with a new awareness: "I beg you. No forgiveness for this or that, for this candle or that insult. Forgive me for being what I am" (p. 195). Not only does Jocelin ask for compassion from his fellow churchman but he also sees how necessary it is to obtain the forgiveness of Roger Mason.

During his final encounter with Roger Mason, Jocelin acknowledges the wrongs he has committed against Pangall, against Goody, and against Roger himself. The priest admits his guilt: "Imagine it. I thought I was doing a great work; and all I was doing was bringing ruin and breeding hate" (pp. 200–201). All Roger can reply is, "You stinking corpse!" (pp. 199, 200, 207). During the course of this conversation Jocelin realizes that he has left Roger a broken man. The master builder, in a speech reminiscent of Peter in *Pincher Martin,* rightly says, "You took my craft, you took my army, you took everything." Jocelin also admits that he contributed to Pangall's death; he confesses his physical attraction to Goody; he reveals that he arranged Goody's marriage, knowing that Pangall was impotent; he even says that he has indirectly killed Goody. Finally, he admits that "I injure everyone I touch, particularly those I love. Now I've come in pain and shame, to ask you to forgive me" (p. 202).

Truly Jocelin's character has changed; he is no longer thinking of Roger as just another object of domination. Once before, he had thought to himself, "He [Roger] will never be the same man again, not with me. I've won, he's mine, my prisoner for this duty. At any moment now the lock will shut on him" (p. 83). In the earlier scene, the "click" of Jocelin's imaginary lock is no different from Pincher Martin's "Eaten!" By the end of the eleventh chapter, however, Jocelin has an increased understanding of his fellow human beings. Though Roger does not give him the consolation of forgiveness, Jocelin's act of seeking compassion signals a significant change.

In each of Jocelin's "debates," irony is the prevailing mode. Leighton Hodson notes that Golding "implies an ironic view of Jocelin's judges who are a pair of gossiping deacons, an envious confessor, and a whore who has lived for gratification of her desires and little else. Their self-deception enriches his basic theme without being heavy handed."[14] Jocelin eventually achieves more insight than either of his two fellow priests, the "petty, legalistic, unforgiving Father Anselm [and] the naive but forgiving Father Adam."[15] Jocelin's interview with Alison only makes him more conscious of his sexual obsession with Goody. During one of his dreams about Goody's fire-red hair, Jocelin says the name "Berenice," unconsciously identifying Goody with the legendary pagan queen, whose hair, dedicated to physical love, was made into a constellation. Ironically, Father Adam, hearing Jocelin speak, assumes he is praying to *Saint* Berenice. When Roger Mason compares Jocelin to a corpse, the paradox of death-in-life, of evil-from-good, of guilt-from-innocence, is dramatically reinforced. Jocelin has assumed that his vision has been inspired by an angel; after his newly gained knowledge, he fears he has been driven by the devil.

FOUR RECURRENT images—those pertaining to phallus, darkness, falling, and flowering plant—all contribute to the multiplicity of meaning contained in the spire itself (the novel is truly "a dance of figurative language,"[16] and at different times the spire is compared to the mast of a ship, a "diagram" of prayer, a dunce's cap, a giant hammer). The four recurring images underscore the pattern of paradox that Jocelin is finally beginning to perceive.

As much as Jocelin represses his sexual passions and as much as he affirms that the construction of the spire is purely a religious goal, the cathedral tower becomes a phallic symbol to him. The spire simultaneously represents the vital life force

and a humiliating reminder to Jocelin that his project is more
a personal demonstration of self than a holy duty to God. The
cathedral is compared to a man lying on his back (p. 4), and the
"very body" (p. 9) of Jocelin's church is adorned with the jutting
spire. The workmen joke about the model of the spire that
Jocelin carries with him: "What an alehouse joke it must seem
to see the dean himself come hurrying out of a hole with his folly
held in both hands" (p. 53). When Jocelin imagines, in a night-
marish dream, that he himself is lying on his back (like the cathedral model) in full view of Rachel, Roger, and Pangall, his fears
are for his own virility. The townspeople of his dream mock him:
"they knew the church had no spire nor could have any" (p. 59).
His further vision of Satan "clad in nothing but blazing hair" sig-
nifies his sexual attraction to the red-haired Goody. Pangall's
physical impotence compares with Jocelin's spiritual ineffectual-
ity. Before the workers drive Pangall away from the cathedral,
they mock him with the model of the spire: "In an apocalyptic
glimpse of seeing, he [Jocelin] caught how a man danced forward
to Pangall, the model of the spire projecting obscenely from between his legs" (p. 84).

Obsessed by sexual longings for Goody, Jocelin turns to the
spire as an outlet for his egotism. The very act of driving the holy
nail into the top of the spire is symbolic of this sexuality. Jocelin
writes in his diary that looking at the completed spire makes his
body vibrate with life, as if a fountain has burst within him, push-
ing up "with flame and light . . . and not to be denied" (p. 816).
In his final dream of Goody, he imagines the "great club of the
spire" rising to meet a tangle of red hair blazing in the sky (p.
213). His last vision of the spire is a sexual one, combining both
masculine and feminine images. This time he imagines that the
spire is "an upward waterfall" thrusting into the sky; yet he also
says it is as "slim as a girl" (p. 215). Jocelin's mixed feelings of
sacred love and physical lust are combined in the shape of the
spire.

The motif of darkness, appearing in *The Spire* just as it has
in the other novels, represents the inner blackness of Jocelin's
soul. Consistent with the paradox of the spire, the black pit that
engulfs the cathedral foundation is contrasted to images of light,

which express Jocelin's most idealistic hopes for the success of his project. The light-dark contrast creates "a *motif* of dual, and sometimes equivocal, significance."[17] The light the workers use during the construction in the darkened church is indirect light, artificially produced by the sheet metal reflector that Jocelin supervises. Corresponding to the cellar image of *Pincher Martin* or the prison cell in *Free Fall,* is what Jocelin calls "the cellarage of my mind" (p. 160). Jeanne Delbaere-Garant has explained this pattern at length:

> Refuge and darkness are now entirely internalized. They are no longer outside man but inside. From man's position in the universe, Golding has focused on a man as a world in itself with the cave and the rock at each of its opposite poles. The pit at the bottom of the cathedral from which Jocelin recoils as the People did from water and Sammy Mountjoy from the wetness in his cell represents the darkness of his own sexuality and lower instincts. This pit in the earth and the woman's womb (Goody's naked belly when she gives birth to her child) . . . [are] seen through the eyes of a man whom centuries of Christianity have taught to distrust all that is "natural" in himself. The cave-cellar-cell has become here the "cellerage" [*sic*] of man's mind, the animality inherent in his human nature.[18]

Jocelin's recognition of his own dark obsessions is expressed through the cellar image: "I'm a building with a vast cellarage where the rats live; and there's some kind of blight on my hands" (p. 202). When he admits to Roger that he arranged Pangall's marriage so that he, Dean Jocelin, could perpetuate his lust for Goody, he uses this same image: "The trouble is, Roger, that the cellarage knew about him—knew he was impotent, I mean—and arranged the marriage" (p. 205).

Though the novel begins with the image of bright sunlight spilling through the stained glass windows, with only a hint of darkness (the unlighted altar), the symbolic setting eventually turns into "a sort of universal black background" (p. 169). By contrast, Jocelin, on his deathbed, desperately seeks some momentary illumination from out of the "panic-shot darkness" (p. 215), and the novel concludes by reversing the pattern of light-dark imagery. The paradoxical symbol of the spire contains the threat of the dark foundations as well as the promise of ascension into the heavens.

The theme of fallen human nature is symbolized by the recurring images of physical falling. The workmen continually risk falling to their death. Early in the novel one worker accidentally slips off the scaffolding, but Jocelin shrugs it off: the workman "left a scream scored all the way down the air, which was so thick it seemed to keep the scream as something mercilessly engraved there" (p. 49). Rachel, Jocelin, and even Roger are all dreadfully afraid of heights. The central suspense of the novel is whether or not the tower will collapse. When some of the stones begin to fall (p. 167), Jocelin fears that Satan is loose. Though Roger insists that the spire cannot stand, it does not fall.

In the last chapter the perspective is changed and Jocelin enters "some new kind of life" (p. 209). Here the imagery complements the idea of epiphany and transcendence. Jocelin is "suspended" in consciousness, as he speaks "wordlessly to himself *above* [italics added] the body" (p. 209). After he admits that he has "traded a stone hammer for four people" (p. 214), he feels the hands of Father Adam "heaving him upright" so that he can breathe fresh air again. But even in his final moments of insight, the old fear returns; Jocelin feels "like a building about to fall."

The vegetation imagery of *The Spire* also contributes to Jocelin's paradoxical revelation in the last chapter. The flowering plant image is a continually changing symbol of both good and evil. It first represents the malignancy within Jocelin's soul. The evil plant is both dying and swelling at the same time: "I am like a flower that is bearing fruit. There is a preoccupation about the flower as the fruit swells and the petals wither; a preoccupation about the whole plant, leaves dropping, everything dying but the swelling fruit" (p. 92). When Jocelin is asked by a board of inquiry to justify his actions, he explains the allegorical nature of his story by using the evil plant image: "It was so simple at first. On the purely human level of course, it's a story of shame and folly—Jocelin's Folly, they call it. I had a vision, you see, a clear and explicit vision. It was *so* simple! It was to be my work. I was chosen for it. But then the complications began. A single green shoot at first, then clinging tendrils, then branches, then at last a riotous confusion" (p. 162). At this point, Jocelin imagines himself "entangled in the tendrils of a plant of sexuality,"[19] figuratively "caught in the branches" of Goody's witchcraft (p. 189).

Second, the plant becomes a symbol of Jocelin's growing obsession with building the spire, at the expense of the human beings around him: "'Growth of a plant with strange flowers and fruit, complex, twining, engulfing, destroying, strangling.' And immediately the plant was visible to him, a riot of foliage and flowers and overripe, bursting fruit. There was no tracing its complications back to the root, no disentangling the anguished faces that cried out from among it; so he cried out himself, and then was silent" (p. 187). Jocelin is unable to confess to Father Adam: "All things were so mixed and the evil plant grew among and over them all" (p. 195).

Third, the image changes to a positive one—the apple tree. In a flash of insight, Jocelin discovers that his spire is like the apple tree: "Suddenly he understood there was more to the apple tree than one branch. It was there beyond the wall, bursting up with cloud and scatter, laying hold of the earth and the air, a fountain, a marvel, an apple tree; and this made him weep in a childish way so that he could not tell whether he was glad or sorry" (p. 196). "The spire-tree in *The Spire* is the outcome of Golding's long-lived obsession and its most perfect poetical transposition. Like man himself, whom it epitomizes, it rises up to the sky away from the gaping pit below, and it owes its vitality to the constant struggle between the upward energy of its stems and the tropism of its roots to the center of darkness."[20]

The spire is simultaneously a product of Jocelin's monstrous ego *and* a timeless inspiration to later generations who will see it only as a successful achievement. It will exist as a monument to God, despite the shabby (but forgotten) motives of its builder. "The spire is beautiful, but compromised like life."[21] Similarly, the apple tree is both a symbol of natural beauty and a reminder of lost innocence in Eden. The apple tree, like the spire, is simple and complicated at the same time. Jocelin has learned that the spire "is built in heavy stone, in faith, in sin; all three things are true, and contradictory."[22]

THE NARRATIVE of *The Spire* allows for interpretations at several levels simultaneously: "For Jocelin there are explanations physiological, psychological, moral, religious, social; all are convincing in themselves; and none is satisfactory."[23] The symbol of the spire does not limit itself to a single "truth." The four levels of meaning particularly relevant to Golding's allegory are: moral, psychological, archetypal, and social.

Thomas McDonnell is justified in calling *The Spire* "Golding's morality play."[24] The novel primarily explores the moral blindness created by Jocelin's "monstrous pride" (p. 184). In addition, Golding considers the implications of a glorious cathedral built for the wrong motives. The interrelationship between good and evil is the central paradox of the last chapter.

From a psychological approach, the narrative discloses the guilt complex stemming from Jocelin's repressed sexual desires. The physical construction of the cathedral spire implies a "corresponding psychological principle."[25] Humankind must acknowledge its own weak foundations (guilt complexes and irrational fears) before it can hope to transcend itself.

The archetypal patterns of the novel are also evident. Jocelin's story embodies the universal quest motif. He seeks to understand himself and his social environment. He is the absurd saint. He shares the role of scapegoat figure with Pangall. After surviving a series of ordeals, he achieves insight into the human condition. He aspires to resurrect his spirit after he has survived the disillusionment of self-knowledge. Jocelin is not only "the Snake struck by the flail beneath the Evil Tree,"[26] but also Adam, who, regretting his pride and selfishness, hopes to achieve forgiveness and regain God's grace.

Finally, Jocelin's story contains social implications. Comparing Jocelin with Oedipus, Bernard Dick observes that "on the human level, each performs an action that ultimately goes beyond personal gain and benefits the community at large—hence the tragic paradox of triumph and destruction."[27] Ironically, and tragically, Jocelin has pushed himself beyond human limits, and has then suffered the consequences of uncontrolled willfulness. That the magnificent spire does stand, however, is partial justification for the audacity of his ambition. Jocelin strives to become something no human can be. His excesses account for his tragedy.

In *The Spire* Golding continues to explore the themes common to his previous novels: that human innocence is an illusion, that compassion is a powerful counterbalance to moral blindness and selfishness, that humanity cannot transcend its condition until it sees itself without deception.

The Pyramid   7

The allegorical implications of Golding's sixth novel, *The Pyramid,* are overshadowed by the emphasis, in this work, on social satire. *The Pyramid* is the most conventionally realistic of the six Golding novels written by the end of the 1960s. It focuses on a specific social environment: Oliver, the protagonist, reminisces about growing up in a small English town in the 1930s. The consensus of critical opinion is that *The Pyramid* signals a new direction in Golding's fiction—a movement toward particularized social criticism and away from allegory.[1] The most severe evaluation has come from Frederick Karl: "*The Pyramid* defies discussion. It is a departure from Golding's other works, lacking their tense, anxious presence. . . . The manner is intended to have serio-comic undertones. . . . The book is a strange agglomerate of shallow intentions and unresolved achievements, almost a throwaway. It adds nothing to our understanding of either Golding or ourselves."[2] Such a statement is incorrect. The novel develops themes common to the entire Golding canon, and also evidences many of the allegorical techniques characteristic of the earlier works.

Only a few critics have detected the several levels of meaning in *The Pyramid.* John Wakeman has called the novel "the most adroitly disguised of William Golding's allegories, and one of the most complex."³ One other critic has noted that "the book is as symbolically dense as any of Golding's previous novels while at the same time dealing more extensively with the contemporary world and exploring new dimensions of characterization and human interrelationship."⁴ Because *The Pyramid* emphasizes a particularized social environment and because the narration is presented through the protagonist's casual reminiscences (rather than through the tormented searches for "significance" of a Sammy Mountjoy), the allegorical implications are more subtle.

The moral allegory of *The Pyramid* is initially suggested by the epigraph from Ptah-Hotep: "If thou be among people make for thyself love, the beginning and end of the heart." The novel demonstrates the failure of the protagonist—as he reflects the twentieth-century condition—to respond to three types of love. In the course of the three sections of the narrative, Oliver barely discovers, without any real alarm, that he cannot experience any spiritual love for Evie, his girl friend from the slums (he reduces their relationship to a physical encounter only); that he cannot accept the friendship of Mr. De Tracy, the pathetic, lonely theatrical man who has been hired to direct the civic musical production; and that he has never felt any "devotion" to Miss Dawlish, his childhood music teacher.

As a social commentary, the novel implies that the entire community (symbolically named Stilbourne), with its severe social hierarchy and its class discrimination, has produced this loveless situation. A pyramid is a tomb, as Marshall Walker has emphasized, and in Golding's fictional town "it is love that is dead and buried."⁵ The problem of free will, one of Golding's major themes, is treated in a decidedly different manner in *The Pyramid*. Oliver's condition is more than a product of his own inner selfishness: it results from the stultifying social environment that negates any free moral choice. "As *The Spire* was about a monument man raised to God, this book [*The Pyramid*] is about the monument man raises over himself: society. Society is exemplified in the pyramidal class structure of Stilbourne."⁶ *The Pyramid*, more than any of the other novels including *Free Fall*, suggests that the external society rather than an inner evil is the source of Oliver's problems. From *Lord of the Flies* to *The Spire,* Golding has implied that a corrupt individual can eventually corrupt his society. In *The Pyramid,* however, a corrupt society impedes individual moral choice.

In *The Pyramid* Golding is again reacting to a literary source, H. G. Wells's *The History of Mr. Polly.* It is not coincidental that "the characters, except for Oliver, are small-town people reminiscent of those in Wells's *Kipps* or *Mr. Polly.*"[7] Golding's own comments on *Mr. Polly* provide the background for the social satire in *The Pyramid*: "I remember a picture that is relevant. H. G. Wells describes it somewhere [in the opening chapter of *Mr. Polly*]. Two radiantly beautiful children, a boy and a girl, clean children, magnificent specimens both, are looking into the dawn. One of those hygienic and comely women who haunted Wells's imagination is kneeling by them, her arm round their shoulders, and she is pointing into the light. She is Education."[8]

Golding sees this picture changing, in the modern world he has come to know: Education "still points into the dawn, but the little girl is yawning; and the boy is looking at his feet."[9] Modern British society hypocritically espouses the high ideals of liberal education, but in reality encourages only those practical vocations that lead to material success. Golding says, "We are like the man who pays lip-service to culture and quiet and meditation; but who shows by his actions that the thing he really believes in is making a fortune."[10] Thus Wells's philosophy of culture, says Golding, yields to "doing" rather than "knowing," and eventually the arts give way to science (Oliver forsakes music for chemistry). The good life becomes a "shaming thing, that we pursue without admitting it." In this new world of material comforts and social prestige, "it is better to be envied than ignored, better to be well-paid than happy, better to be successful than good—better to be vile, than vile-esteemed."[11]

The society of Golding's childhood in Marlborough was greatly different from the Wellsian ideal, but noticeably similar to the fictional community of Stilbourne. In his autobiographical essay, "The Ladder and the Tree," Golding has commented that in "the dreadful English scheme of things at that time, a scheme which so accepted social snobbery as to elevate it to an instinct, we [the Golding family] had our subtle place."[12] The "social tight-rope" that young Golding was forced to walk is the same one that Oliver describes in *The Pyramid.* Oliver, however, is not so aware of the moral implications of such class snobbery. He is, in fact, an unknowing victim of the social hierarchy.

The Pyramid does not mark the first time Golding has writ-ten about a "social pyramid." In *Free Fall,* Sammy Mountjoy con-siders his "adoption" by Father Watts-Watt to be an opportunity for instantaneous prestige: "My anomalous position in the rec-tory gave me a rootless background so that I boasted in compensation—boasted with rudimentary feeling for the shape of our social pyramid that I was the rector's son, sort of."[13] In his essay, "Egypt from My Inside," Golding uses a similar figure of speech when discussing modern society's celebration of science to the exclusion of all else: "We are not, for all our knowledge, in a much different position from the Egyptian one. Our medi-cine is better, our art, probably not so good; and we suffer from a dangerous pride in our ant-like persistence in building a pyra-mid of information. It is entertaining information for the most part, but it does not answer any of the questions the Egyptians asked themselves before us. And we have a blinding pride that was foreign to them."[14]

The idea of the pyramid prescribes the three-part organiza-tion of Golding's novel. Though the symbolism is not as elabo-rate in *The Pyramid* as it is in the earlier novels, the interplay of agents, action, and imagery is directed by the allegorical nature of Oliver's narrative.

PROPER NAMES in *The Pyramid* contribute to the symbolism. The name of the town is the most obvious example: "In *The Pyramid,* Golding is now a social myth maker; he has progressed from a mythical universe (The Coral Island in *Lord of the Flies*) through mythical heroes (Lok, Pincher Martin, Jocelin) to a mythical community with a name so transparent that it needs no commentary—Stilbourne."[15] Even critics who argue that the novel is not allegorical concede that the name for the town makes an appropriate comment on Oliver's loveless, socially fixed community.[16]

Character names are particularly fitting. The adolescent Oliver views his two girl friends as contrasting types: Imogen, beautiful and idealized, is consistent with her Shakespearean counterpart in *Cymbeline*; Evie, earthy and sensual, is identified with Oliver's loss of innocence. Oliver continually stresses this duality: "Evie had none of Imogen's sacred beauty. She was strictly secular."[17] When he daydreams about Evie naked, he unconsciously thinks of Imogen, but quickly catches himself, "appalled at having even inadvertently equated the two of them" (p. 43). It is clear to the reader, however, that the primary difference between the two is social.

In the second section of the novel, Norman Claymore is revealed to be as superficial as the image that his surname connotes. Evelyn De Tracy's sarcastic manner is reaffirmed by the association with Evelyn Waugh. Miss Dawlish, though gradually pushed into eccentric behavior, is fundamentally as "dullish" as her name suggests. Her musical tastes (p. 158) are as limited as her talent (pp. 141 and 164). The church voluntaries she dutifully practices are, according to Oliver, characterized by "impeccable dullness" (p. 174). She "teaches music as she inherited it, as boredom."[18] The particular connotations that Oliver associates with each character, and by which he identifies the townspeople as social types, are reflected in the nomenclature.

In each of the three sections of the novel, a state of nature is shown to be analogous to a state of mind. Each state indicates the progress of Oliver's psychological development. Evie triggers in him a new awareness of his own sexuality, and in his adolescent enthusiasm he imagines that the very woods surrounding the town have become alive with sex: "I looked up at the slope to the escarpment with its cascading rabbit warren, its alders, and, beyond them, my clump of sexy trees at the top" (p. 60). Oliver's new feelings affect his perspective of his physical environment. The "dark, sexy woods" (pp. 34, 59, 77, 79) tell us about his inner state rather than his outer world.

The second section reveals the collegiate Oliver. During his first term at Oxford, Oliver has been exposed to the neat equations of science and the security of the rationalistic philosophy. He wishes to find "answers to life" that are logical. He naively informs Mr. De Tracy that life is "like chemistry" (p. 123). He becomes increasingly frustrated, however, when he encounters life situations that do not fit logical patterns.

In the last section, as Oliver grows in his awareness of the complexity of human beings, his picture of Miss Dawlish becomes as dark and unclear as the shadows that engulf her house. When she emerges from her darkened room to march through town wearing nothing but her hat and gloves, Oliver observes her from behind his own dark brick wall. His mind is a whirl of confusion and ambivalence; he does not know whether to mock or to sympathize. He compares his sense of emptiness and uncertainty to a spider web: "There was a storm in me which felt as if it were around me, so that the dry webs of spiders between the bricks seemed part of it and of her and me, and everything" (p. 175). His understanding of the old music teacher remains as tenuous as the spider web, an image also connoting the dry lifelessness of the woman herself.

The single instance in which the narrative invites comparison with an extrafictional event occurs when Oliver sees himself as a guilt-ridden Adam. As a result of his sexual affairs with Evie, he laments his fallen state, wishing that "the days of our innocence might return again" (p. 81). The comparison is ironic, for Oliver is only concerned about his sexual guilt and what his father will say; the young man disregards his own callousness to Evie. She has not seduced him; he has dominated her. She is a mere object to him, and he maintains his social aloofness throughout their relationship. His egotism and his lack of human understanding constitute a larger moral dilemma than simply his loss of virginity. Though he melodramatically refers to Evie as "this fallen woman," it is he himself who has succumbed, both to the class prejudices of his town and to his own selfishness.

Each of the three sections of the novel presents an analogy by which a recurring action manifests Oliver's inner state of mind. His characteristic laughter when confronted with the opportunity to express human compassion demonstrates the insensitivity that so flaws his personality. His response to Evie after they have made love for the first time is to laugh in her face (p. 56). Oliver is exhilarated by "the pride of possession" after his affair with Evie. He feels nothing else. Evie confesses that her lecherous employer, Captain Wilmot, has threatened to beat her at the slightest provocation, but Oliver merely laughs (p. 61). When he later discovers Evie's welts, he is dumbfounded. Then he assumes that the truth is "plain to see," connecting the welts with Captain Wilmot, but forgetting about the girl's belligerent father, whose "meaty fists" and short temper are well known.

The unreliable narrator says, "Kneeling there, then, staring at her, and not seeing her but only the revelation, the pieces fell into place" (p. 71). He has never really "seen" her, or he would have understood what precipitated her earlier willingness to be "hurt" (p. 62). Oliver only stares "without seeing her" (p. 72), and then reacts characteristically: "I think my first sound was some kind of a laugh of sheer incredulity. Then I could see her. . . . I laughed again" (p. 72). When he next looks at her, she is again reduced to a mere "object" (p. 73). "She wanted tenderness," Oliver observes, "So did I; but not from her. . . . She was the accessible thing" (p. 71).

With Mr. De Tracy, Oliver is similarly unfeeling. He is oblivious to De Tracy's admission that "I have a great deal of woman in me, Oliver" (p. 121). In response to Oliver's quest for the truth, the theatrical man produces pictures of himself dressed as a woman. Oliver bursts into laughter (p. 124). The rejected De Tracy says no more. Oliver notices that his friend has "moved away," though De Tracy continues to sit at the same table. The boy's inebriation accounts for this distancing effect, but the scene also communicates De Tracy's sense of alienation. Oliver laughs again (p. 125) and then makes his way back to the civic theater. Later when he puts the hopelessly drunken De Tracy on a bus back to Barchester, Oliver is still laughing (p. 129).

Oliver's experiences with Miss Dawlish reveal the same pattern. An honest attempt at human understanding is met with uncomprehending laughter. On one of the few occasions when the aging music teacher abandons her severely masculine clothing for a frilly dress, Oliver suppresses a laugh: "it did not take [her eyes] long to read the incredulity in mine" (p. 154). At her graveside, a more mature Oliver surprises himself when he openly mocks Miss Dawlish's memory: "I caught myself up, appalled at my wanton laughter" (p. 180). Oliver's recurrent laughter in reaction to Evie, Mr. De Tracy, and Miss Dawlish is an index of his own lack of humanity.

OLIVER'S PROGRESS toward self-knowledge is, like Ralph's (in *Lord of the Flies*) and Christopher's (in *Pincher Martin*), involuntary. The persons he encounters remain mysteries to him, but when he begins to sense his own ambiguous feelings about Miss Dawlish, he achieves a new level of human compassion. Oliver also acquires self-knowledge, which eluded him before. His description of his childhood memories could well apply to the pattern of the novel: "I . . . sort my impressions into two piles—one of primary, ignorant perception; the other a gradual sophistication" (p. 138).

Though Oliver's reminiscences are less intense than Sammy Mountjoy's announced search for his lost freedom, the very nature of the narration in *The Pyramid* establishes the quest motif. Oliver undergoes the physical journey of returning home (the first two episodes are focused on his returns from college; the last section describes his return to Stilbourne in 1963, after many years have passed).

In the first section, the collegiate Oliver has been away three years, but there is little change in his attitudes. Contrary to Thomas Wolfe, Oliver *can* go home again: "I had returned, with a sophisticated nostalgia to assure myself that I could no longer enjoy the pleasures of childhood, and was finding with a mixture of irritation and amusement that I was in danger of enjoying them thoroughly" (p. 83). Two years earlier, during his freshman year, he had returned with an intense longing to find in the familiar surroundings of Stilbourne some meaning for his life. This is the Oliver who declares to Mr. De Tracy, "I want the *truth* of things. But there's nowhere to find it" (p. 123). In the last section, as Oliver drives into town, he finds himself rethinking his past experiences in Stilbourne: "My hands turned the wheel of themselves, and without conscious intention I found myself gliding down the

spur to all those years of my life" (pp. 131–32). When he meets
Henry and is told of Miss Dawlish's death, he only half-listens:
"I was busy examining myself" (p. 134).

The epigraph for the novel introduces the theme of love, a
motif that is satirized by Evie's gold cross inscribed *Amor vincit
omnia*. But love is crucial to Oliver's moral predicament, in that
he cannot unselfishly concern himself with other persons. He can
have sexual intercourse with Evie, but he cannot love. At those
times when he honestly evaluates his feelings (specifically in the
final section of the novel), he admits his limitation: "I examined
my heart for emotion but found none" (p. 132). His reaction to
his hometown is to think "critically, but without much feeling"
(pp. 134–35). As a result of the confrontations concluding each
section of the novel, Oliver achieves a limited knowledge of the
major characters—Evie, Mr. De Tracy, and Miss Dawlish—and an
increased insight into his own heart.

The battle motif is established by the three confrontations.
In the first dialogue-debate, Oliver meets Evie on his return from
college. She is a prostitute living in London, and she too has returned to Stilbourne for the annual fair. In the course of their
meeting in the tavern, Evie reminds Oliver of his own guilt: "It
all began when you raped me" (p. 89). The reader is reminded
of her earlier denunciation of Oliver: "You wouldn't care if I was
dead. . . . And I'm damned and you're damned with your cock and
your cleverness and your chemistry" (p. 70) (the speech could
have been directed to a Pincher Martin or a Sammy Mountjoy).
As Evie's rage mists Oliver's spectacles during the heated dialogue in the tavern, the young protagonist is provided with a puz-
zling revelation. For the first time Oliver sees Evie as a human
being in her own right: "It was as if this object of frustration and
desire had suddenly acquired the attributes of a person rather
than a thing" (p. 90). He discovers that she is capable of just as
much frustration as he is, and that she has suffered much more
acutely the pains of class discrimination than Oliver was aware.
In a burst of emotion, Evie confronts Oliver: "*You!* Aren't you
ever going to grow up? This place—you. You an' your mum and
dad. Too good for people, aren't you? You got a bathroom. 'I'm
going to Oxford!' You don't know about—cockroaches an'—

well" (p. 90). Then she reveals her own sexual guilt, which stems from a sadistic relationship with her father. Oliver must rethink his prior assumptions about Captain Wilmot, for Evie has revealed a complexity of anxieties that the boy had never suspected: "I went home confounded, to brood on this undiscovered person" (p. 91). In this last scene with Evie, he has also been reminded of his own willfulness and class snobbery.

As a result of Oliver's conversation, in the same tavern, with De Tracy,[19] the protagonist sees Imogen and her husband for the petty, class-conscious, pseudo sophisticates that they are. Oliver says that such knowledge makes him feel "free" (p. 129).[20] The photographs of the producer in ballerina costume remain a mystery to young Oliver, but the accumulation of such mysteries is contributing to the humanizing process that Oliver is undergoing. The final scene of the novel indicates that Oliver is considering with new insight how the lack of love and a sense of desperate isolation can explain the most eccentric human behavior.

Oliver's scene at the graveside of Miss Dawlish marks the most dramatic confrontation. First, he reminisces about some of the moments of Miss Dawlish's frustrated lovelife, moments that meant little to him at the time: the frilly dress (p. 154), the muffled sobs in a darkened room (p. 168), the defiant nakedness (p. 175). Oliver has noticed the daily conflict between Henry Williams's mechanics and Miss Dawlish's music—the pitched battle between technology and the arts. In his later life, Oliver has opted for Henry's practicality: "like Henry, I would never pay more than a reasonable price" (p. 183).

Oliver's immediate reactions to Miss Dawlish's memory merely indicate his own conventionality. The great surge of protective love that he feels for his daughter, as he compares her potential happiness to the wasted life of Miss Dawlish, is a pat reaction: he is fiercely determined "that she [his daughter] should never know such lost solemnity but be a fulfilled woman, a wife and mother" (p. 179), as if "fulfillment" automatically evolved from marriage. Oliver, however, does experience moments of more penetrating insight.

First, he is reminded of his mother's mockery of Miss Dawlish after the old music teacher has marched naked through the town: "I . . . was consumed with humiliation, resentment, and a sort of stage fright, to think how we were all known, all food for each other, all clothed and ashamed in our clothing" (p. 173). Furthermore, when Oliver discovers the ashes of music, he recognizes how ironic are the words on her tombstone: "Heaven is Music." For Miss Dawlish, music was a hell—a frustrating substitution for love. Oliver has surprised himself by admitting that he really hated his old teacher, but what he hated was what he feared in her—the blackness of a loveless life.

Another important revelation for Oliver is his feeling of compassion for Miss Dawlish, despite his denunciation of her only minutes before. Her bitterness and alienation, revealed by the ashes of all her musical memorabilia, haunt Oliver's mind: "I sat on her chair, put my elbows on my knees and my face in my hands. I did not know to what or to whom my feelings had reference, nor even what they were" (p. 182). To Oliver, Miss Dawlish's life of quiet desperation emphasizes the ambiguities and mysteries of the human predicament. One is reminded of Golding's own fascination for the ancient pyramids. To Golding, the pyramid is a special symbol: "Man himself is present here, timelessly frozen and intimidating, an eternal question mark."[21]

THREE PATTERNS of imagery—pertaining to excrement, blackness, and music—reinforce the symbolism of *The Pyramid*.

The recurring images describing filth and excrement symbolize Oliver's underlying feelings of moral guilt. Oliver righteously deplores the squalor of Evie's slum neighborhood: "the cottages got progressively smaller, meaner, dirtier, and more decayed" (p. 40). He assumes that such filth is merely an outward manifestation of the moral corruption of the poor. After his shameless sexual conquest of Evie, however, he associates images of the cloaca with himself. Oliver's severe class consciousness, not any sense of personal ethics, is responsible for his guilt feelings. Though he laments his sordid romance on an earth that smells of decay— "life's lavatory," he calls it (p. 73)—he continues to make love amid the rabbit dung (p. 77). He recognizes his physical loss of virginity but does not admit to any loss of moral values. His only fear is condemnation from his parents: "I stood, a heap of dung, yearning desperately for some sewer up which I might crawl" (p. 81). Oliver's later memory of his isolation in the darkness of Miss Dawlish's water closet also incorporates this imagery.

Dominating many of the scenes in *The Pyramid* are images of blackness. This recurring imagery figuratively represents the lack of spiritual love, the deficiency that affects all of Stilbourne. The furtive attempts at sexual lovemaking must be hidden in the dark woods. Oliver considers Evie to be simply an "object" to be used, and the shadows encourage such exploitation. At first, Oliver thinks that Evie's dark eyes are sensual; when he later confronts her at the fair, her black eyes and mouth make her look like a corpse (p. 89).

The loveless Miss Dawlish surrounds herself in darkness (pp. 139–40). She exists "in a dark emptiness, [in] a house empty of life except for the grinning piano" (p. 150). Oliver's childhood experience in Miss Dawlish's water closet recalls the cellar-cell images in Golding's prior three novels. The blackness of Miss Dawlish's house, however, is not a manifestation of her lurking inner evil as much as a metaphor for her loveless isolation. Like Evie, Miss Dawlish has a terrible darkness in her eyes (p. 170). Her only companion is a cat who appears to enjoy the silent darkness of her house (p. 178). Returning to this empty house years later, Oliver searches his heart for sympathetic feelings for his former teacher, but is caught up in the sinister atmosphere: "as if unnameable things were rising round me and blackening the sun, I heard my own voice ... crying aloud. 'I never liked you! Never!'" (p. 180).

Images associated with music are closely identified with the theme of love. In Stilbourne, however, the social disharmonies are reflected in the lack of genuine musical feeling throughout the community. Furthermore, "the combination of music and love takes on symbolic significance, opposing the exaltation of science represented mainly by Oliver's father."[22]

Images from music unify the three sections of the novel. When Oliver fights the doctor's son for the prize of Evie, the skirmish is ironically described in musical terms: "I hit him with my octave technique, fortissimo, sforzando, in the pit of the stomach. It was lovely" (p. 20). Evie's jazzy singing of "boop-a-doop, boop-a-doop" contrasts with Oliver's practicing of Chopin. The snob-bish Oliver dismisses Evie's interest in popular music as merely more evidence of the bad taste of her class (pp. 34–36). Oliver's piano playing is more an athletic exercise in frustration than a mode for loving expression. For the loveless Evie, who has turned prostitute, there is truly no reason to sing any more, not that the respectable civic theater had ever asked her. When Oli-ver asks if she still sings, she answers, "Who? Me? Whatever for?" (p. 85). Particularly significant are Oliver's final thoughts of Evie. Viewing her as a human being for the first time in his life, he belatedly senses that they might have had a basis for a more meaningful love relationship: "as if I might—as if *we* might—have made something, music, perhaps" (p. 90).

Each recurrence of such imagery underlines, by contrast, the social disharmony of Stilbourne society. In the second section of the novel, Oliver's participation in the civic musicale ends in comic disaster for the amateurish company. In the final section, music for Miss Dawlish is a hateful ordeal because of her father's dictatorial influence. Eventually the music becomes a daily re-minder of her lonely, isolated life: "She had become one of those cases on which Stilbourne turned its corporate back" (p. 175). The music motif fittingly dramatizes Oliver's loveless world of Stilbourne.

The Pyramid, while concerned with the moral significance of Oliver's life, provides a different emphasis from the earlier Golding novels. It explores the extent to which a particular *social* environment affects a person's capacity for moral choice and even defines personality. Nevertheless, Golding's method of pre-sentation is shaped by the allegorical techniques that character-ized his previous work.

8 The Later Novels

Darkness Visible

The major focus of my study is on the first six Golding novels. Though each offers a different artistic emphasis or subject matter, all six suggest a kind of homogeneity in that each work embodies a modern moral allegory. Furthermore, a dozen years would elapse before the publication of *Darkness Visible.* In the first half of the present decade, Golding's novels are gravitating toward twentieth-century settings (*The Pyramid* pointed the way here); they are more openly concerned with the injustices of the British class system, and they are incorporating an ironic humor to make some of their points. Though the later novels still include allegorical elements, they reveal a more flexible use of symbolism within specific social contexts.

In the first chapter of this book I observed that Golding's novels blend the realistic with the symbolic, and *Darkness Visible* is no exception to that general pattern. This novel offers both social realism, like *The Pyramid,* and moral allegory, in the style of the novelist's most abstract fictions. It is a marvelous illustration of the simultaneous presence of the fabular and the factual, so characteristic of all Golding's work.

Just when Bernard Oldsey had pronounced Golding a victim

of "future shock," and destined for some kind of post-"cult figure" oblivion,[1] *Darkness Visible* appeared, though to extremely mixed reviews. On the one hand, Brad Owens objects to "this old-fashioned allegory of good and evil" and says that Golding has committed the ultimate literary sin: "he has written a boring book."[2] By contrast, John Batchelor overreacts and declares the novel to be Golding's "masterwork," his highest writing achievement,[3] strong praise for what appears to be Golding's most abstruse work. The general pattern of criticism is familiar, and most succinctly expressed by the ubiquitous Joyce Carol Oates, who sees Golding as a writer of "pristine allegory," a vehicle employed "mainly to instruct, to teach; our habit with vehicles is to disembark once we have reached our destination."[4] Thus she does not think that Golding's novels bear rereading and regrets that "the allegorical mode triumphed" in *Darkness Visible.*

The tendency toward moral allegory is first established by the title of the novel itself, which alludes to Milton's powerful vision of the Fall in Book One of *Paradise Lost:* "A Dungeon horrible, on all sides round/As one great Furnace flam'd, yet from those flames/No light, but rather darkness visible." We are immediately on familiar ground for Golding readers: focus on the Fall motif; the prevailing image of darkness; the concern about the nature of evil. The epigraph from Book Six of Virgil's *Aeneid* extends these themes further, as the dark powers are evoked: "Grant me to tell what I have heard! [With your assent / May I reveal what lies deep in the gloom of the Underworld!]".[5] Though Golding will again explore the nature of evil, his focus remains in the real world. Milton's flaming furnace will become Golding's London under siege during World War II, and the fiery scene concluding the novel will bring the story full circle, from one fiery event to another.

Though Milton and the Bible form the literary backdrop for *Darkness Visible,* many other influences are evident. Oates sees Iris Murdoch; Benjamin DeMott mentions parallels with Thomas Hardy; Doris Grumbach is reminded of the crazed evangelists of Flannery O'Connor; Batchelor notes a correspondence with J. C. Powys; Owens discusses Golding and Dickens; Frank Tuohy sees a kinship with Melville.[6] We soon discover that Golding's new novel is considerably larger in scope and setting than the earlier works. First, the book spans almost four decades in England, from the tense war years, to the mild 1950s, to the drug-culture sixties (and Gerry's little black pills), and finally to the terrorism of the seventies. Second, it not only offers four fully developed major characters—Matty, Sophy, Sim, and Pedigree—but scores of secondary figures, giving the novelist a chance to depict character by way of the quick vignette or telling conversational phrase.

Like *The Pyramid, Darkness Visible* is an allegory that demonstrates the loss of love and its consequences, but the theme never becomes so abstract that we forget about the explicit social context of the setting. All of Golding's favorite themes are here: the breakdown of love (and the indirect reminders to the reader concerning the desperate necessity of that love); the lack of communication (and the resultant human alienation); the relative degrees of evil; the problem of balance or control (a Euripidean theme).

In a general sense, there may be events in the novel that have an autobiographical frame of reference, but I resist the idea that the book is "an allegory of the man William Golding," an allegory that discloses how the author's "young hopes were scarred by war's terrors, how he was a schoolmaster, how he sought the source of man's guilt in the prehistoric as Matty turned to earth's most primeval humans, how he drowned Pincher Martin, built a church spire, wrote in notebooks."[7] Golding's purposes are larger than this. When he told Professor Tiger that he wanted to write a novel "not about Britain, about England,"[8] he was envisioning a story that would include London during the war, the history of Frankley's (implying the social-economic development of all England), and even the modern legacy of terrorism as current as the headlines of today's newspaper.

The most important structure of *Darkness Visible* is the multiple ironies that inform nearly every page. Though many critics see Matty as a religious champion, surely his "heroism" has to be qualified at every turn. Similarly, other major characterizations are affected by Golding's ironic view.

The personified agents in *Darkness Visible* are first developed through nomenclature. Matty's name is most obvious. If we think of him as hopelessly naive in the ways of the world, and obsessed to the point of religious fanaticism, then he is not much of a "gift of God," as his name translates. Still clearer is the significance of "Matthew Seven,"[9] as he is called in the early days, suggesting the New Testament text that begins: "Judge not, that ye be not judged. For with what judgment ye judge, ye shall be judged." This invokes the idea of compassion and understanding which, for example, help clarify the final scene in the park, when Pedigree is "judged." That Matty's surname is continually changed or misunderstood adds a kind of universality to his character, yet it also comments on the problem of communication and identity (in a manner reminiscent of the character named Chance in Jerzy Kosinski's *Being There*).

Just as "Greenfield" seems particularly inappropriate for a town overrun by jet noise, rumbling trucks, disparate racial groups, dispossessed church yards, and relocated cemeteries, so irony affects many of the character names. Mr. Stanhope is totally void of any hope or love. Mr. Goodchild, who assumes that "Stanhope's little girls were everything to each other" (p. 102), could not be more wrong about them; Sophy is not the "good child" Mr. Goodchild imagines her to be. Sophy's misanthropy hardly makes her "wise," as her name translates; she has been blinded by her obsession with "Weirdness." Fido Masterman is master of nothing; indeed, Sophy leads him around like a dog. Eventually Masterman is relegated to the state of helpless hostage. Mr. Pedigree's pedigree is pederast. And the odd-job man who announces Henderson's death is devilishly named, of all things, "Merriman."

The most obvious correspondence of a state of nature with a state of mind is the opening war sequence, the London holocaust that becomes a symbolic landscape of the world condition. In eight pages, Golding offers a view into hell. World War II, as we have already seen, was the single most important factor in shaping Golding's outlook on life, and his estimation of human beings. In those opening eight pages, we are back with Milton again. The blinding, "shameful, inhuman light" (p. 11) is a tangible expression of the manmade nightmare of war. This is the realm of Conrad, Kafka, Hawthorne. Ironically out of this conflagration comes the child—godliness from the burning bush? The angelic from the fiery furnace? Golding's opening scene defines the dimensions of his art: the natural scene is charged with symbolic force.

In *Darkness Visible,* irony complicates the connections between certain natural phenomena, like physical appearance, and state of mind. The character most closely associated with godliness and asceticism is a ghastly, misshapen grotesque, while the most sinister evil presence in the novel—Sophy—is a beautiful woman, to the outside world.

The primary extrafictional events in *Darkness Visible* are the many biblical analogues. The curious events in Matty's life establish the absurd saint motif. He is much like Ezekiel of the Old Testament. The Book of Ezekiel begins with a vision of fire, consistent with Matty's wondrous genesis. His ordeal with the wheels (p. 74) reminds us of Ezekiel's vision of the angelic wheels, a literal response to Ezekiel 1:16–21.[10] The vengeance against Edom, introduced in Ezekiel 25:14, is the same curse that is later alluded to when Henderson is killed. In both Psalms 60:8 and 108:9 we read, "over Edom will I cast out my shoe." Though Golding's text is not clear about the exact circumstances of Henderson's death, for Matty's shoe is found under the body, and Matty under interrogation can only mumble the verse from Psalms (pp. 35–36), there is an ironic implication established. Presumably Matty is connected with Henderson's fall, after literally "casting his shoe" at the suspected wrongdoer. In this regard, Matty's fanaticism and blind literalness do great harm (just as Sophy's monomania does).[11] Matty, however, will have the opportunity for redemption through sacrifice.

Matty becomes the absurd Christ figure, as he is baptized in the swampy water (p. 75); chides himself for dishonesty in his journal entries (when he enters "6/6/66" he says "so that not to make a lie of it the number should be 7/6/66" [p. 89], and similarly he wants the reader to know he did not ride his bicycle up the hill, but rather "that would be a lie, I pushed my bike up" [p. 97]); has holy discussions with spirits concerning the purchase of his bike; and undergoes the wildest crucifixion and emasculation imaginable. This is, no doubt, fulfillment of Matthew 19:12

(p. 61) the hard way. The outlandish confrontation in the suburbs of Australia, with the aborigine Harry Bummer (Golding is having more fun with names) is the most preposterous scene in Golding's novels.[12] It tops Pincher Martin's efforts to give himself an enema, while imagining heroic background music. When the narrator lapses into mock King James cadences, the comic effect is achieved: "And Matty came in the evening unto the city of Gladstone which is a great city. And he sojourned there for many months at peace, finding work as a grave-digger" (p. 60).

The fourth technique for intensifying allegorical agents—the manifestation in an action of a state of mind—is best illustrated in Sophy's sadistic willfulness. A female Pincher Martin, Sophy takes pleasure only from inflicting pain or controlling others. She kills a duckling and experiences a long "pleasure" (p. 109); as a young child she practices "willing" the movements of others (p. 132); she talks to the ex-soldier Bill only in order to find out what it is like "killing people" (p. 155); she achieves sexual orgasm only after she has stabbed her partner with a knife (p. 147); she revels in manipulating Fido (p. 164).

Similarly, though more subtle, Matty's implication in Henderson's death—a death that the saintly boy has naively caused in his blindly literal reading of the Bible—suggests that a fanatic's commitment to "good" can also have negative results. His pilgrimage and suffering are tinged with guilt feelings of unworthiness. Ironically both Sophy and Matty are linked together in their extremism, for they share a common fanaticism. Whether revealing her sadism or his righteous indignation, both their actions are connected with death and symbolize the extremities of their spiritual positions.

The journey and battle motifs particularly apply to Matty, who travels throughout four decades as he continually tries to determine his purpose in life. His constant question, "What am I and what am I to do" (p. 99), is a central preoccupation with all Golding's major characters, from Simon to Sammy to Jocelin. Ironically, Matty's final sacrifice seems more accidental than revelatory.

The battle pattern is only implied, since Matty and Sophy directly meet only once (p. 182), though at that time even the dull-witted Matty senses her evil. Though the two characters are treated separately throughout much of the novel, a clear dialectic is established. Matty believes God determines all acts; Sophy sees only chance. Matty, through his talks with the spirits (reminiscent of the inner monologues of Jocelin), strives for transcendence; Sophy merely believes in the principle of entropy (pp. 131 and 166). Matty is physically ugly, but inwardly (though naively) good; Sophy is pretty, but covertly evil. Matty seems unreal, both in his appearance and in his contemplations. Sophy is absolutely too real. We cannot be certain that she does not speak for a whole generation.

What these two figures have in common, however, is the passion of their extremism. "Golding's characters are always caught up in a cataclysm of excess. 'Nothing in excess' is the motif that runs through his favorite tragedian, Euripides. It is also the key to the world of William Golding."[13] In *Darkness Visible* a kind of moral blindness affects both Sophy *and* Matty. It is what precipitated Henderson's death; it is what plotted the kidnapping. As Derwent May has observed: "The idea that seems to emerge from the story . . . is that deprivation of love breeds fanatics, that they may be fanatics either for good or evil, yet in either case they streak a path through the world that alone can show up the full drama of man's life in a religious universe. They make 'darkness visible,' but they also hint at the nature of true light."[14]

Virtually all the major characters experience isolation and are unable to love effectively. Sophy is indifferent to sexual matters; any notion of "love" is replaced by sadism. "Love" is a "four-letter word which she never used" (p. 152, 154, 185). Furthermore, an incest theme is introduced at the end of part 2 (p. 186). It is also clear that Matty shuns any physical contact with women, fleeing in confusion at the sight of the seven Hanrahan girls (p. 59). Sim Goodchild eventually admits to himself that his interest in the young Sophy was unwholesome (p. 224). Edwin Bell's love life is rumored to be frustrated; Edwina, his wife, is more masculine than he is (p. 198). Mr. Stanhope, through his succession of "aunties," in his hateful conversations with Sophy (p. 140), and in his pronouncements about the triviality of sex (pp. 186–87), offers another example of thwarted love in the novel.

Pedigree is the clearest illustration of unnatural love, yet there is truth to his contention that he has not hurt the children, but only himself (p. 265). His pitiful situation of loneliness, frustration, and fear gets little attention, though he has earned the hate of the entire community. Yet his sin is not Sophy's, by any stretch of the imagination. It is an index of Golding's compassion as a writer that we can sympathize with Pedigree's circumstances. His anguished "help me" (p. 265) achieves a level of awareness that only Sammy Mountjoy and Dean Jocelin have attained. Again, the necessity of forgiveness becomes central to any final vision from the darkness. The switch to the scornful park keeper's point of view dramatizes the way the inner and outer worths of a human being are often at odds.

There is one central pattern of description that affects every page of *Darkness Visible*—the light-dark imagery. It is contained in the oxymoronic title of the novel, and early in part 1 the narrator expresses the major theme that focuses the symbolism: "People find it remarkable when they discover how little one man knows about another. Equally, at the very moment when people are most certain that their actions and thoughts are most hidden in darkness, they often find out to their astonishment and grief how they have been performing in the bright light of day and before an audience. Sometimes the discovery is a blinding and destroying shock. Sometimes it is gentle" (pp. 29–30).

It is not necessary to trace all the many references to light or darkness in the novel. We remember the "shameful, inhuman light" of the wartime London streets; the child in the burning light described as "apocalyptic" (p. 15); the parable of the bushel and the candlestick, which Matty likes to recite (p. 55); the bright otherworldly spirits described in Matty's journal; the fire at the boys' school, Sophy's very "own fire—a thing she had done, a proclamation" (p. 250); the fiery confrontation of Matty and Bill (p. 248); and Pedigree's final golden revelation in the park. The light is sometimes evil, more often good, but its meanings must be rethought every time the imagery appears. Light is associated not only with destructive fires but with purifying visions. In *Darkness Visible,* the light encompasses both Sophy's terrorism and

Matty's mysticism, and it seems particularly fitting that the same, common image is used to underline these paradoxes.

Rites of Passage

In some respects *Rites of Passage* belies its historical setting and seems as immediate and direct as anything Golding has yet written. Though the author obviously enjoys establishing an unreliable narrator—Edmund Talbot, a pretentious ass who demonstrates his class snobbery and insensitivity at every turn—and re-creating the pomposities of late eighteenth-century literary style, the novel squarely addresses itself to modern social issues: the hypocrisies of love, the tyranny of rigid class divisions, the crisis of a workable religious view. Don Crompton believes that the accessibility of *Rites of Passage* makes it even more contemporary than either *Darkness Visible* or *The Paper Men,* "being more concerned than the other two (for all its historical setting) with everyday life, the 'ordinary universe' in which most people live most of the time."[15]

For the most part the novel has been well received by critics, many of whom are still reeling from the labyrinthine ways of *Darkness Visible.* Characteristically, the most skeptical critics have had reservations about the convention of the sea journey: they think they smell allegory. Jean Strouse considers the novel to be a recycling of the scapegoat motif (drunken sailors substituted for murderous schoolboys): "Its effects seem contrived. This journey into another heart of darkness has the feel of a rerun."[16] Nereo Condini is more blunt: "As the umpteenth allegory of the ship as microcosm it limps. It sounds more like the Gospel according to John explained by Evelyn Waugh to a group of Rotarians."[17] Other critics explain to the readers that the "allegory" does not get in the way of a good story: "We have been treated to a rattling good yarn, whether we attended to the allegory or not."[18] Robert Towers recognizes that *Rites* is a novel of ideas, but also anticipates that at any "hint of allegorizing I can imagine a shudder passing through certain prospective readers. But they need not fear. Though there is indeed a schoolmasterish streak in Golding, inclining him toward the didactic, tempting him to embellish his work with literary references (to the *Ancient Mariner*) and echoes (of Conrad and Melville), he has in *Rites of Passage* constructed a narrative vessel sturdy enough to support his ideas."[19]

Though *Rites of Passage,* with a title suggesting archetypal levels of meaning and a setting in the isolated microcosm of a ship at sea, would ostensibly lend itself to symbolic action, much of the novel revels in the comic characterization of the obtuse narrator. Indeed, Golding refers to the book as a black comedy: "I think the book ought to be viewed much more as an entertainment. . . . I thought a lot of it was just funny."[20] Though Talbot tries to be both witty and wise, so that he can report to his patron the detailed facts and "acute observations" about the voyage, he constantly mistakes what is really happening, never understands anyone's motivation, and remains unaware that some of the passengers are talking about him when he hears Miss Granham say, "let us hope he learns in time then!"[21] The alcoholic Brocklebank (at the Captain's table), the ridiculous Colley (in his first appearance to Talbot), the oversexed Zenobia—all offer delightfully comic moments.

In one typical scene, Talbot, after invoking the name of Nelson, describes his personal victory at sea: a sexual coupling with the steamy Miss Zenobia, accompanied by the collapse of his bookshelf:

> We wrestled for a moment by the bunk, she with a nicely calculated exertion of strength that only just failed to resist me, I with mounting passion. My sword was in my hand and I boarded her! She retired in disorder to the end of the hutch where the canvas basin awaited her in its iron hoop. I attacked once more and the hoop collapsed. The bookshelf tilted. *Moll Flanders* lay open on the deck, [and] *Gil Blas* fell on her. . . . I struck them all aside and Zenobia's tops'ls too. . . . We flamed against the ruins of the canvas basin and among the trampled pages of my little library. We flamed upright. Ah—she did yield at last to my conquering arms, was overcome, rendered up all the tender spoils of war! (p. 86)

Certainly there are serious themes developed in *Rites of Passage,* but the high spirits of its comedy (though mostly black) consti- tute much of the artistic impact here.

Some of the character names suggest added dimensions of irony. If "Edmund" owes its etymological origin to the idea of "wealthy protector," we see in Edmund Talbot someone who longs after the prestige of wealth, but one who could not even protect his own personal dignity, much less defend anyone else. Neither can he protect his social naiveté nor his moral indiffer- ence. As the story progresses, he is forced to recognize, if only temporarily, his own shortcomings. Zenobia makes a rather floozy queen, more the aging whore than a royal presence (if the name conjures up thoughts of the third-century queen of Pal- myra). Mr. Prettiman has a name that connotes the smugness of his rationalist viewpoint, though Golding purposely makes him look more humorously absurd than some of the other rationalists of earlier novels (Piggy, Pincher, Pringle). At one point Prettiman stands on deck with a blunderbuss, hoping to shoot down any passing albatross and thereby put an end to the romantic super- stitions created by Mr. Coleridge's poem. Even Talbot observes that Prettiman "demonstrates to the thoughtful eye how really ir- rational a rationalist philosopher can be!" (p. 73). James Colley's initials, "JC," suggest a Christ parallel, and indeed he functions as an absurd saint figure, one who is more comically naive than simply innocent.

Other character names are less significant: Wheeler, the quiet, mysterious servant who can supply virtually every need, including opium, is a "wheeler-dealer" of sorts; the character who offers the most positive demonstration of strength and good sense is named Summers; and Billy Rogers, foretopman, a not-so- innocent young seaman who is involved in the investigation about Colley, recalls Melville's Billy Budd, though Golding has often denounced any such similarities. In an interview with Her- bert Mitgang, Golding proclaims, "Nothing in common to Budd at all, nothing. No possible similarity ever occurred to me. Any- way, this chap in my novel doesn't get hanged."[22] In a later inter- view with James Baker, Golding adds, "I thought this Billy had

absolutely nothing in common with the other Billy. He is diamet-
rically opposite. He is corrupt. He is the opposite of innocence
in every conceivable way."[23] Yet when Baker asks him if he had
that contrast in mind, Golding admits he did. The irony of Billy
Rogers's characterization makes an effective contrast with Melville.

There are ways in which the natural world of the sea setting
parallel certain states of mind. Not only are the characters isolated in space and time on board ship, but their physical
separation—in their cabins, in the off-limits areas proclaimed by
the captain, by the "line" that is not to be crossed—corresponds
to their human isolation. Their physical separation suggests a
similar social (even more than spiritual) alienation. Captain Anderson seems to enjoy the privileges of his position and the
"power of isolating a man from his fellows" (p. 142), but we
know he is a tyrant. Colley initially retreats to his cabin in humiliation, speaking only irregularly to Summers and the servant Phil-
lips. Eventually the minister literally wills himself to death in the
isolation of his cabin. Both Talbot and Colley remark about the
claustrophobic gloominess of their cabin rooms, and as the story
unfolds, we soon see how Colley's world of naive religion and
Talbot's world of social arrogance make them more isolated from
one another than either could ever imagine.

The physical circumstances of the seasickness of both Colley
and Talbot can be seen as an outer manifestation of the inner
social ills (particularly in Talbot's case), which create an underlying tension. Similarly the fact that their ship literally stinks because of the sand and gravel ballast (p. 5) would be an appropriate symbol for the inner chaos of the passengers. Just as Jocelin's
church is built on swampland, so Talbot's ship is filled with rot-
ting ballast. Talbot observes that the passengers themselves "shall
shake down—presumably in the way the sand and gravel has
shaken down, until—if I may judge by some of the passengers—
we shall stink like the vessel" (p. 8).

Apart from the characterization of Colley as an absurd Christ
figure (providing a biblical analogue for purposes of irony),
there are explicit references to Plato, Aristotle, Richardson, John-
son, Milton, and Sterne, among others. However, there are three
other extrafictional referents, from classical, romantic, and mod-

ern literature, respectively, that expand the meaning of the text. First are the several references to Homer, reminding us of the great sea journeys in the *Iliad* and *Odyssey,* where ancient heroes rise to mythic proportions as they demonstrate their powers within the context of national epic. The dramatic contrasts with Talbot's situation extend the irony. He invokes a conventional Homeric metaphor when they begin their journey "over the broad back of the sea" (p. 34), as he cites the Greek to a stupefied crewman, Willis, who replies that he does not know French (p. 35). Every time Talbot waxes literary, whether referring in Greek to the fear of Pan (p. 75) or the "meaningless faces" of the passengers (p. 122), we are reminded of a heroic classical literature of sea journey that dwarfs the presumptuous Talbot and his journal at every turn.

Second is the comparison to Coleridge's *Mariner.* This would seem the most obvious literary parallel. The poem is referred to by Talbot and even quoted by Zenobia (p. 59). References to Coleridge's poem can serve several purposes: they establish a romantic sensibility that could be viewed as one of the central conflicts between the eighteenth-century Talbot and Rev. Colley, a hapless mariner whose romantic notions of the sea will eventually contribute to his downfall. They recall the conflict between Christian and pagan forces, ones that Colley will also have to confront. Finally they reinforce the symbolic journey of a "soul," not only Colley's but also Talbot's. Though the plot of the novel focuses on Colley's initiation, it is Talbot's movement toward self-knowledge (and the realization that he has not actually known the truth of matters) that is at the heart of the book.

Third is the suggestion of Conrad's *Heart of Darkness,* particularly when, after discovering the facts surrounding Colley's death, Talbot decides to lie to Colley's sister about what has happened, much as Marlow does to Kurtz's intended: "I shall write a letter to Miss Colley. It will be lies from beginning to end. I shall describe my admiration for him. I shall record all the days of his *low fever* and my grief at his death. A letter that contains everything but a shred of truth! How is that for a start to a career in the service of my King and Country?" (p. 277). A symbolic sea voyage, the look into the face of evil, a destructive personal withdrawal ending in death, the narrator's decision to lie about what happened—all of this makes a strong identification with Conrad. Though Golding admires Conrad, he has, however, grown quite tired of the inevitable comparisons:

> I think I'm pretty much tired of being asked which story of Conrad['s] I got which of my stories from. I'm pretty much tired of always being told how much I owe to *Heart of Darkness.* I read that book *after* I wrote *Lord of the Flies!* I admire Conrad immensely for his word painting of sea-scapes and sea scenes and his shipness. I don't really much care about the rest. There are so many novels that one can't spend one's time caring about other people's novels, otherwise you go right up the wall, at least I should.[24]

The most direct illustration of a plot action corresponding to an inner state of mind is the drama of Colley's death. He literally wills himself to death, as the ultimate manifestation of guilt, a personal yet pathetic response to sinfulness. Rather than affecting a black veil, like the minister in Hawthorne's story, Colley simply starves himself to death. Based on an actual historical incident described in Wilfrid Scawen Blunt's diaries and also in the first volume of Elizabeth Longford's biography of the Duke of Wellington—a book Golding has read[25]—*Rites of Passage* fictionalizes events surrounding a real-life parson traveling by ship from India to the Philippines. Golding has stated: "I found that it was necessary for me, for my peace of mind, to invent circumstances in which it was possible for a man to die of shame, you see?"[26] A more subtle instance of a plot action that parallels a state of mind is Talbot's willingness to write a false letter to Colley's sister. This decision reveals a softening and humanizing of his moral disposition, an act (like Marlow's) motivated by a desire not to compound the suffering and humiliation of others. But obviously Colley's self-willed demise is much more symbolically dramatic.

The two major patterns of allegorical action—progress and battle—are certainly evident in *Rites of Passage.* First, the sea voyage immediately establishes the journey motif. The word "rites" of the title suggests a literal passage from an old world to a new one (England to Australia in this instance). It also brings to mind the ceremonies associated with "crossing the line" on board the ship, as well as the initiation that both Colley and particularly Talbot experience as they achieve a bitter self-knowledge. The romantic Colley refers to the ship as a world unto itself: "It is as if I think of her as a separate world, a universe in little in which we must pass our lives and receive our reward or punishment" (pp. 191–92). He regularly calls the ship "our little world" (p. 190), or the area not off-limits to himself as "my *kingdom*" (pp. 209–10). It is only a matter of time before kingdom turns to prison (p. 230). At any rate, the setting of the lonely ship at sea is consistent with the way Golding has isolated his characters in previous novels. Talbot deemphasizes the clock-date of his departure when writing his patron: "The date? Surely what matters is that it is the first day of my passage to the other side of the world" (p. 3). And it is not long afterward that Talbot "finds himself adrift in an allegorical sea of lies, doubts, and false assumptions that we call normal behavior," as Golding offers us a "shattering study of the bounds of moral responsibility."[27]

Second, the battle motif is established, early in the book, as a conflict between Talbot and Colley. Talbot is almost instinctively repelled by the silly parson, granted that their first meeting involves Talbot's being covered by Colley's vomit! Talbot gives us a comic description of Colley's physical awkwardness (p. 15) and clownish appearance (p. 42). Talbot recoils at the minister's obsequiousness and can barely hide his displeasure. Colley "opened the door to me and made his usual sinuous genuflection. My dislike of the man returned" (p. 64). Talbot, with his eighteenth-century disposition and political ambitions to serve the state, contrasts with the romantic Colley, who is identified with the church and who counters Talbot's rationalism with his own religious position. Talbot's aristocratic sensibility is irritated by Colley's democratic, missionary zealousness.

Though Colley is openly more silly than Talbot, both men are naive about the ways of the real world. By not recognizing the rigid social proprieties of class and not understanding the pagan world of the sailors, Colley makes bad personal judgments that lead to an unbearable guilt; ironically, his predicament develops from his commitment to religious values. Colley is defeated by his own weaknesses, and much like Hawthorne's ministers who have seen the nature of evil, he cannot cope with his own guilt. On the other hand, Talbot, though not in such a life-and-death situation, is at least capable of changing for the better. By reading Colley's letters he begins to develop a sympathy for the parson and a recognition that he, Talbot, has met Colley's sincere overtures of friendship with icy social aloofness. It also gradually occurs to Talbot that he has misunderstood much of what has happened during the voyage. By the end of the novel, he is less sympathetic to the haughty Deverel; he discovers the sexual disgrace of Colley's situation; and, most importantly, he recognizes how his own friendship with the parson could have made a major difference in the turn of events. Colley is no longer viewed as an adversary.

Nonetheless, it is misleading to characterize Talbot as a completely changed man. His insights about the human condition and the importance of compassion are temporary at best. As he reaches the end of his story, he is still preoccupied with "scoring" points in conversation (p. 275); he still mistakes the identity of the "sailor hero," the writer of love notes to Zenobia (p. 273); he still is oblivious to the criticism of others and assumes they are talking about Summers (pp. 275–76); he is still just as pretentiously literary as ever, as he offers a final quote from Racine (p. 278). His closing lines do indeed sound like Marlow: "With lack of sleep and too much understanding I grow a little crazy, I think, like all men at sea who live too close to each other and too close thereby to all that is monstrous under the sun and moon" (p. 278). But one sentence cannot nullify the whole characterization being established in the last chapter of the novel. Talbot's "insight" must be qualified. It is not so clearly a change from naiveté to realization, as Grove Koger believes,[28] or a passage "from arrogance and condescension to compassion and understanding," as Vincent Balitas asserts.[29] Talbot cannot shed a lifetime of bad habits, but it is fair to say that he is at least beginning to perceive the realities of the human predicament and that now he is not so hasty to condemn others.

Two major patterns of imagery dominate this novel. First of all, images of filth connected with vomit and excrement function symbolically to underline the idea of a prevalent inner human sickness, an evil within. Golding has used this technique before, but in *Rites of Passage* the imagery dealing with excrement and vomit contributes to a satiric, almost Swiftean, effect of deflating particular characters. Colley's first reported act is one of vomiting against the wind (p. 15) and eventually befouling Talbot (p. 16). When Colley makes what Talbot characterizes as a typically "sanctimonious remark," Zenobia answers, "Amen!" while her father responds more crudely with "a resounding fart from that wind-machine Mr. Brocklebank so as to set most of the congregation sniggering like schoolboys on their benches" (p. 69). Later, in a drunken stupor, Rev. Colley "turned to his right, walked slowly and carefully to the bulwark and pissed against it. What shrieking and covering of faces there was from the ladies, what growls from us!" (p. 117). Directly after that, Colley blesses them all.

More seriously, the "badger bag," which plays a major part in the sailors' mock ceremonies, is filled with dirty, foul water. Colley writes that just "when I thought my end was come I was projected backwards with extreme violence into the paunch of filthy water" (p. 238). He notes that he harmed no one, yet those in the crowd are merciless in their lust for punishment. Their behavior is evil personified: "Yet now as I struggled each time to get out of the wallowing, slippery paunch, I heard what the poor victims of the French Terror must have heard in their last moments and oh!—it is crueler than death, it must be—it must be so, nothing, *nothing* that men can do to each other can be compared with that snarling, lustful, storming appetite" (p. 238).

The other pattern of imagery draws on the metaphor of the stage or theater. In a world (if only on shipboard) where persons are not what they seem to be, where words perpetuate class distinction and social discrimination, where love is superficial illusion or perverse humiliation, it is fitting that Talbot is increasingly aware of the dramatic, theatrical quality of social conventions. He recognizes that Zenobia's affected, exaggerated speech owes more to the theater (p. 58) than to any desire for accurate communication. When Talbot speculates about his wicked desire to link Zenobia with Colley, to have fun at both their expenses, he sees life as a mere play, an amalgam of Platonic shadows lacking substance in themselves: "I examined the train that had led me to such gross thoughts and found its original in the dramatic nature of Zenobia's appeal—straight back to farce and melodrama—in a word, to the theatre!" (pp. 102–3).

Golding has used images of the theater in other works, notably *Pincher Martin* and *The Pyramid,* in addition to publishing a comedy, *The Brass Butterfly.* In the setting of a ship's journey, the many references to theater in *Rites* not only reinforce notions of the discrepancies between appearance and reality, but also hint at the superficiality of creatures playing at real-life roles. Talbot further notes, "Even if I refuse to disgrace myself by it, I cannot, it seems, prevent the whole ship from indulging in theatricals!" (p. 104). He concludes that life seems more like Italian farce than Greek tragedy, determined by the lack of dignity of modern protagonists. He sees the physical layout of the ship as a giant theater (p. 109). The events in plays, however, seem simple and straightforward compared to the mysteries and confusions of life: "I was never made so aware of the distance between the disorder of real life in its multifarious action, partial exhibition, irritating concealments and the stage simulacra that I had once taken as a fair representation of it!" (p. 110).

On one occasion, he confuses clock time with the artificial time in a theater: "During—it may be—half a minute; for what is time in a ship, or to revert to that strange metaphor of existence that came to me so strongly during Mr. Colley's exhibition, what is time in a theatre?" (p. 129). When trying to create a scenario of the Anderson-Colley affair, Talbot refers to the ship as "our floating theatre" (p. 145), at a point where he is not sure about the boundaries between truth and conjecture. Even Colley defines his authority by the vestments he wears, simplistically confusing the outer with the inner. Golding has commented on the dramatic quality of *Rites:* "It had to be theatrical because he [Colley] had to make an exhibition of himself, and therefore the ship had to be turned into a theatre in which he could do it."[30]

It would appear that the preoccupations of this novel are more contemporary than its historical setting would suggest.

Again the theme of homosexual love is introduced, almost as a contrast to the petty, hypocritical sexual intrigues of Talbot. Again the subject of class distinctions is prominent. As Talbot discusses the difficulties of translation, Mr. Summers soberly comments: "In our country for all her greatness there is one thing she cannot do and that is translate a person wholly out of one class into another. Perfect translation from one language into another is impossible. Class is the British language" (p. 125). Much of the conflict in the novel stems from such social rankings.

And again, but in much more direct manner than in *Darkness Visible,* Golding injects a great deal of humor into his narrative. This all prepares the way for his most openly comic work, *The Paper Men,* published four years later.

The Paper Men

William Golding's *The Paper Men* is a striking contrast to his earlier work. Its strong autobiographical elements, its departure from the allegorical-symbolic mode often associated with Golding's novels, and its bitter humor represent a new emphasis in the Nobel Prize winner's fiction.

First of all, rather than using an isolated island setting (as in *Lord of the Flies* and *Pincher Martin*) or distancing his subject in a remote historical period (as in *The Spire* or his novel of "prehistory," *The Inheritors*), Golding has set his story in the present, as he humorously focuses on both the current literary scene and particularly the academic world. Though some of Golding's earlier novels have had a modern setting, *Free Fall* and *Darkness Visible,* for example, depend on World War II experiences for much of their texture, and the extended reminiscences of *The Pyramid* deemphasize the current time frame.

The Paper Men tells the story of an aging, mean-spirited, alcoholic English writer named Wilfred Barclay, who is insecure about his fading talents, contemptuous of the literary scene that awards undeserved fame and fleeting fortunes, and alienated from his family because of his own egotism and insensitivity. He is hounded throughout the novel by a young American scholar, Rick L. Tucker, who wants to become Barclay's official biographer and literary executor, mostly for the purpose of achieving tenure.

Barclay recoils at becoming a mere cog in the great machinery of American scholarship and flees from Tucker's meddling. No matter where Barclay runs, as he travels all over the world to escape the constant badgering by his would-be Boswell, Tucker is never far away.

Though the despicable Barclay is obviously not Golding, there may be some intentional self-parody here. Prior to *The Paper Men,* Golding's novels have contained little of what could be called recognizable autobiographical material. But with this new work, he almost devilishly patterns the career of the snide, morally reprehensible Barclay after events in his own life. Barclay, like Golding, is a bearded,[31] aging English novelist, who lives in an old house in the country, outside of London literary circles. He occasionally writes for British literary magazines; Barclay, like Golding, has contributed to the *Times Literary Supplement* (p. 115). He is a "church fancier" (p. 26) in a manner reminiscent of Golding in his essay "An Affection for Cathedrals."[32] He has had some inconsequential stage experience and then went off to the war, just as Golding did. He has traveled widely and has particularly enjoyed driving his own car in the States, while on a two-year "academic merry-go-round" (p. 26); Golding once stated that he rented a car after his Hollins College residency in 1962 and drove along the entire West Coast. He also enjoyed extensive driving in North Africa, as does Barclay in *The Paper Men* (p. 25). Barclay's first novel, *Coldharbour,* is an instant success and keeps on selling (p. 24), much as continued sales from Golding's first novel, *Lord of the Flies,* insured enough financial security for him to quit teaching and devote himself to full-time writing. Finally, both Barclay and Golding reject the idea of any biography being written about them. Critic Virginia Tiger, in her book *William Golding: The Dark Fields of Discovery,* has supplied a brief two-page summary of major events in Golding's life, but she first acknowledges that he has "requested that no literary biography be written" and adds, "One must honor the spirit of this request."[33]

Over the years, Golding has expressed his uneasiness with Academe. He has written some delightfully satiric pieces in the "Westward Look" section of his essay collection, *The Hot Gates,*[34] in which he sympathizes with the black lawn-keepers who are treated as invisible men at Hollins College in Virginia, a place where liberal arts do not include changing racial stereotypes. He pokes fun at the superficiality of creative writing classes, where precious analysis of the psychological motivation of fictional characters substitutes for hard work or masks the lack of student talent.

In Golding's "Foreword" to his book of interviews with Professor Jack Biles, he tells about an informal reception for him after one of his lectures at an American university:

> I was colloquial and witty; or, at least, those round me seemed to think so, laughing, as they balanced their cups of coffee. At last the party broke up; and just as I was about to leave, a young man appeared at the door, walked straight towards me, ignored me, bent down, extracted a tape recorder from beneath the seat I had just vacated, and disappeared through the door again. Now the most depressing aspect of this episode was not the tape recorder—since I was used to seeing them wherever I went—but the look in the eye of the young man who owned it. He was on the job. His eyes were set. His jaw and, indeed, his course were set. He had just the look of a man going busily down to the river for a bucket of water.[35]

In his book of essays called *A Moving Target,* Golding laments that "for better or worse my work is now indissolubly wedded to the educational world. I am the raw material of an academic light industry."[36] On the one hand, he is flattered, but on the other, he recognizes the drawbacks, particularly "postgraduate students in search of a thesis."[37] Wilfred Barclay refuses to let Tucker become the "Barclay man," but not just because of the artificiality of fabricating a biography that will perpetuate the socio-historical game-playing of later critics, nor because Tucker is an ass, the stereotype of a single-minded opportunist who values Barclay's work only as a potential passport to his own career security. Barclay actually rejects Tucker because any detailed biography will reveal the unpleasantness, infidelities, and ugliness of his own all-too-shallow life.

At any rate, in *The Paper Men* Golding has incorporated autobiographical elements that he had previously shunned.

Second, Golding has moved far away from the familiar techniques of modern allegorical literature, techniques he adopted in the past: the use of names to function symbolically, the comparison of a state of nature with a state of mind, the introduction of an extrafictional frame of reference outside the story itself, and the connection of plot action with a state of mind. Ever since Golding's twelve-year hiatus after writing *The Pyramid* in 1967, he moved slowly but steadily away from the allegorical patterns of his early works. *Darkness Visible,* with its study of the fanaticism of both good and evil, and *Rites of Passage,* with the sea voyage ending in the increased if only partial insight of its narrator, allow for allegorical possibilities, but both works are considerably more flexible in their symbolism than Golding's first six novels.

In *The Paper Men* the allegorical pattern is simply not realized in any systematic way. Names do not figure significantly, though one critic, in observing the titles of some of Barclay's novels, notably *All We Like Sheep,* is reminded of a passage in Isaiah, prophesying the coming of Christ.[38] The natural, physical setting of the novel does not figure prominently in Golding's story. The only plot event that recalls an extrafictional frame of reference is the appearance of stigmata on Barclay's hands and feet as he undergoes a kind of religious epiphany near the end of the novel. There is a brief scene in which Barclay is "saved" by Tucker from falling over a steep cliff. Actually, because of the night and the thick fog, Barclay does not realize that he is only a few feet from the ground, and that Tucker's efforts to "save" him are unnecessary. It surely would be straining matters to view this scene as symbolic of the meaningless, artificial relationship that links academics to artists, and hence a connection between an action and a state of mind.

However, this is not to say that some of Golding's major concerns are absent from *The Paper Men.* All Golding's novels deal with the evils of selfishness and the exploitation of others. In one ghastly scene, Barclay makes Tucker literally beg like a dog. The professor is pathetic, but Barclay, at that point, unknowingly damns himself. Many of Golding's characters typically suffer from the blindness of self-deception, and Barclay is no exception. For him there is eventually no place to escape. Though he thinks of the American as shallow and exploitive, Barclay is slowly becoming linked to Tucker in a doppelganger relationship recalling the writings of Kafka or Poe. "Broad hints are dropped that the author and the critic have begun to exchange identities."[39] Their accents are moderating, Rick taking on British inflections and Barclay flattening his intonations (p. 138). Barclay's dying wife tells him what he has only begun to guess: "You know what? You and Rick have destroyed each other" (p. 175). In addition, Golding's novels underscore the need for human compassion and sympathetic understanding, but ironically any change of disposition in Barclay will come too late in this novel.

Finally, in *The Paper Men* we find more sustained humor, however bitter and sarcastic, than in any other Golding novel. Normally one of the least humorous writers of the contemporary British novel, Golding has fun creating Barclay's cynical commentary—a commentary always delivered at the expense of the groveling Tucker.

Many of the jokes are directed at the academic world. Rick L. Tucker, an assistant professor at the University of Astrakhan, Nebraska (which he calls "Ole Ashcan"), is not above literally going through Barclay's trash in order to salvage material for his research. He even offers Barclay his rather dense but pretty wife, Mary Lou, in order to win favor. Mary Lou explains how they chose Wilfred Barclay for Rick's specialty: "He said no one else was doing you as of this moment in time. . . . He couldn't find anyone. He did look, Mr. Barclay, Wilf, because I did too. I was his student, you know. We worked together on you, sir. He said in that kind of study you can be beaten by a nose. . . . He said he was investing our time and money in you—Wilf—and we couldn't afford to make a mistake" (pp. 64–65). Mary Lou has not read any of Barclay's work, but she knows the titles of everything he has written. When he asks her how this is so, Mary Lou replies, "I majored in flower arranging and bibliography" (p. 65).

The first time Barclay ever meets Rick is at a meeting of scholars, most of whom (including Barclay himself) are dozing while Rick reads his paper:

What jerked me awake was the sound of my own name in Tucker's peculiarly toneless American. His head was down, and he was reading from the manuscript, and he was on about my relative clauses. He had counted them, apparently, book by book. He had made a graph, and if they consulted appendix twenty-seven among the goodies handed to them by the grace of the conference organizers, they would be able to find his graph there and follow his deductions. . . . Prof. Tucker, still toneless, was now pointing out the significant difference between his graph and the one constructed by a Japanese Professor Hiroshige [who] had not done his homework, to our surprise, and had also been guilty of the gross error of confusing my compound sentences with my complex ones. (p. 23)

Though Rick has never met Barclay, the young professor claims he knows the author personally, but during the course of his pronouncements he happens to look up from his reading and sees Barclay himself in the audience. Rick goes into shock, tries to ad lib, turns two pages at once, and then drops his entire manuscript, while Barclay slips out of the room. Later on in the novel, Rick admits to Barclay that as an undergraduate he once got a friend to put a tape recorder under the novelist's chair at a school reception, in order to get a sample of his diphthongs for Rick's phonetics class. (We remember Golding's own true story.)

Toward the end of the novel, Barclay tells the professor that he, Wilfred Barclay, is going to write his own biography, and that he is going to write Tucker into it too. According to Barclay, Rick makes the appropriate response of a frustrated academic: "Rick gave a kind of howl. I've never heard anything like it. Perhaps it's how a wolf howls or a coyote or something strange and wild. Things got very confused after that. I mean he also kneeled down or rather flung himself down on his knees. He also bit my ankle" (p. 182).

Golding's comments in an earlier essay that uses the imagery of a moving target are particularly appropriate to Wilfred Barclay's situation in more ways than one. After receiving a letter from a young woman who was looking for a subject on which to do her graduate thesis, Golding learns that her professor had suggested that she focus on a figure from the past:

> He had recommended her to do a thesis on someone who had known Dr. Johnson—in fact, on *anyone* who had known Dr. Johnson. However, she was an advanced student and knew that everyone who had known Dr. Johnson was now dead. You can, I suppose, guess what she was after. She was not going to write a thesis on anything as dull as a dead man. She wanted fresh blood. She was going out with her critical shotgun to bring home the living. . . . I wrote back at once, saying that [she should] find someone who had known Dr. Johnson. . . . . She could guarantee filling him with a shower of critical small-shot at any time *she* wanted. But as for me, I am a moving target.[40]

Appraisals of a Writer in Progress   9

Though the last three Golding novels suggest new directions for their author, his novels are, for the most part, remarkably unified in their themes and techniques. Each of the narratives, with the exception of *The Paper Men*, which moves away from the allegorical mode, is an analogical expression of the novelist's moral concerns. A central theme in Golding's work is that exploitation and selfishness signal the end of individual freedom and the beginning of human misery. The breakdown of democracy in *Lord of the Flies,* the flight into darkness by the fear-ridden Homo sapiens at the conclusion of *The Inheritors,* Pincher Martin's self-made hell, Sammy Mountjoy's lost freedom, Jocelin's monomaniacal obsession that destroys himself and the lives of four others, Oliver's muddled recognition that he has contributed to the alienation of three other persons—all of these situations emphasize the theme of exploitation.

Second, the novels dramatize the idea that self-deception is a more common condition than self-awareness. Few of Golding's characters realize that evil originates from within the human heart rather than from without. Though the protagonists often gain self-knowledge unwillingly and only as the result of painful conflict, the motif of the quest is integral to all the novels, particularly *Darkness Visible* and *Rites of Passage*.

Third, the importance of human compassion, the ability to seek forgiveness as well as forgive, is a major theme in Golding's novels. The humble act of asking another human being for help, of looking beyond oneself, is what distinguishes Sammy Mountjoy from Pincher Martin, or Dean Jocelin from Jack Merridew.

Fourth, the conflicts between the humanistic and the scientific, between culture and technology, between the spiritual and the rational, are central to Golding's allegories. The dualities symbolized by Piggy and Simon, Nick Shales and Rowena Pringle, Oliver's father and Miss Dawlish, reflect this conflict. The neat "answers" the rationalists provide are ultimately not satisfying to either Sammy Mountjoy or William Golding.

In all his novels Golding is defining ethical behavior. In the first two novels, the morality of a society is shown to be dependent on the integrity of the individual. The fall of Ralph's society in *Lord of the Flies* or the rise of Homo sapiens in *The Inheritors* are manifestations of collective human evil. In the next three novels, Golding is concerned with varieties of religious experience, "proceeding from Pincher Martin, who attempts to deny everything not fathered by his ego, through Sammy Mountjoy, who is capable of visions informed by divinity, to Dean Jocelin, who learns to acknowledge his guilty self and seeks to abandon it."[1] In the last four novels, Golding reexamines the problem of ethical behavior in society, but this time finds that the social environment can be an evil in itself, though modern terrorists are a considerably more serious subject than tenure-track professors.

In my discussion of Golding's moral allegory, I have intended to clarify the major themes of each novel. The tropological significance of Golding's work, however, does not account for his achievement as a *novelist*. Apart from the moral allegory, Golding's poetic use of language, the texture of irony that subtly pervades his novels, and the refinements he has made in characterization—all these features provide added dimensions to the writing.

In discussing each of the novels, I have noted Golding's

striking use of imagery. The easy manner in which Golding moves from simile to metaphor is another facet of his poetic technique. In *The Pyramid*, Oliver first mentions that Evie's eyes are "like black plums," and afterward they are simply called "the plums": "The plums glanced up at me over her hands" (p. 6). The same device is used to describe Pincher's skull as "the center" or Goody Pangall as simply "the hair." This technique by which "the epithet unites with the object has a timeless, almost epic quality about it and must have been the way in which poetry originated—from an essential oneness between the poet and his natural environment."[2]

Fundamental to Golding's novels is irony. First, in many of the works, Golding has reacted to literary sources that then become ironic foils to his own novels. Second, each novel introduces an ironic point of view. The problem of the reliability of Golding's protagonists is always crucial. The most dramatic instance of this is Lok, whose simple Neanderthal consciousness is the frame of reference for *The Inheritors*. But Pincher Martin does not perceive his actual condition; Jocelin is as blind to his moral state as any protagonist in Greek tragedy; Oliver is too concerned about himself to understand the persons around him; Matty's religious monomania distorts his knowledge of the real world; Edmund Talbot is preoccupied with social station; and Piggy does not really know what has happened to the boys any more than the naval officer does. Golding's well-known shifts of viewpoint in the final chapters of his novels also contribute to the irony, though the conclusion to *The Paper Men* is the most predictable.

The gradual development of Golding's skill in characterization has culminated in *Darkness Visible*. Because his allegories have stressed ideas more prominently than characters, the protagonists in his early novels have been rather one-dimensional. However, he has continued to narrow his focus from a group of schoolboys to a smaller group of Neanderthals to the single characters of Pincher, Sammy, and Jocelin. Such limiting has produced refinements in the characterization of the protagonist.

In *The Pyramid* and *Darkness Visible,* however, the secondary characters are just as interesting as, and also somewhat more complex than, either protagonist, Oliver or Matty. Evie and Miss Dawlish represent two of Golding's most effective women characters; Sophy is his most complex female. Golding has simply not supplied enough detail for the characterizations of Fa or Goody Pangall, and Beatrice's standard reply of "maybe" is no equal to the mixture of coquettishness and frustration that together define Evie. Sophy's characterization takes its place with Pincher Martin as one of those enigmatic figures combining strength of will with evil self-indulgence. In addition, the vivid and expansive cast of major and minor characters in *Darkness Visible* is sufficient indication that Golding need no longer think of himself as a novelist "more interested in ideas than in people."[3]

The Pyramid has signaled new directions for Golding and the last three novels have explored these new areas at greater lengths. First, the recent novels dramatize the corruptions of heterosexual love contrasted with a kind of strange innocence associated with homosexual love, as if Golding is standing on its head that large subject (love) and any conventional expectations about it. The pattern was first established in Golding's story "Clonk, Clonk," which posits a race of homosexual, innocent males contrasted with heterosexual, guilty females.[4] In *Darkness Visible,* the sadistic destructiveness of Sophy seems much more an evil than the pathetic Mr. Pedigree. In *Rites of Passage,* Talbot's hypocrisy with Zenobia is less honest than anything Rev. Colley does.

Second, there is a movement toward twentieth-century settings, and a more direct consideration of how class distinctions represent a kind of incurable social disease. Even *Rites of Passage,* set in the early nineteenth century, seems contemporary in its focus on social criticism.

Third, and most different from the tone of the early novels, there is more open humor in these later novels. The absurdities of Matty's shoe-throwing or his Australian epiphany, the pomposity of Talbot and the silliness of Colley, and the Barclay-Tucker relationship (satirizing academic life)—all of these situations have no equivalents in the earlier works, whose guarded optimism was qualified by some rather grim ironies.

In one respect, it is unfortunate that Golding's career began with the celebrated *Lord of the Flies,* a work that is more conventional in theme and structure than his other novels. The eight other, but less well known, novels more clearly reveal the sophistication of Golding's imaginative powers. In responding to the question of whether or not an artist has the responsibility to communicate to his audience, Golding has said:

> I think one of the things that's the matter with us, surely at the moment, is that almost anything that is not worth saying can be said with infinite clarity and anything which is worth saying can only be put across in a special kind of thought-way which hits people at many levels and says to them, "Now look here, this is not a Coca-Cola advertisement, this is not a pronouncement by the Senate or the President or the Queen or whatever, this is a particularly relevant set of communications being made to whoever can grasp it."[5]

The "many levels" of Golding's allegories have been the subject of my study. As the 1983 Nobel Prize reaffirms, Golding's nine novels have established him as a serious, highly original artist whose work has enriched modern literature.

Notes

Chapter One—Allegory and the Modern Novel

1. Robert Scholes, *The Fabulators*, p. 11.
2. C. Hugh Holman, W. F. Thrall, and Addison Hibbard, *A Handbook to Literature*, p. 13.
3. Robert Kellogg and Oliver Steele, eds., *Books I and II of "The Faerie Queene*,*"* p. 7.
4. William Golding, "Fable," in *The Hot Gates and Other Occasional Pieces*, p. 94.
5. James Keating and William Golding, "Purdue Interview," pp. 191–92. Golding also admits to being a moralist in a later interview with Jack I. Biles—*Talk: Conversations with William Golding*, pp. 86–87.
6. William Golding and Frank Kermode, "The Meaning of It All," p. 9. This important interview is also published, in part, in Baker and Ziegler's casebook, already cited, pp. 197–201.
7. Biles, *Talk*, p. 7.
8. See John MacQueen, *Allegory*, p. 1: "From the beginning . . . allegory has been closely associated with narrative. All western and many eastern religions have found their most perfect expression in myth—a narrative, that is to say, or series of narratives which serves

to explain those universal facts which most intimately affect the believer, facts such as . . . moral laws, the sense of inadequacy and failure and the sense of potential, both of which characterize the greater part of mankind."

9. See Angus Fletcher, *Allegory: The Theory of a Symbolic Mode*, p. 16n, who quotes from Coleridge's *Essays and Lectures on Shakespeare and Some Other Old Poets and Dramatists*.

10. See Paul Piehler, *The Visionary Landscape: A Study in Medieval Allegory*, pp. 1–20. For a further discussion of the "double force" of medieval allegory, in which the "thing understood" evolves from the "thing said" but both function simultaneously, see Thomas C. Niemann, "'Pearl' and the Allegorical Mode," in "'Pearl' and the Medieval Christian Doctrine of Salvation."

11. Virginia Tiger, *William Golding: The Dark Fields of Discovery*, pp. 24–27.

12. See, for example, MacQueen, *Allegory*, in which some half-dozen modes and "levels" of allegory are discussed, including mythological, narrative, figural, situational, numerological, and psychological varieties. Surely Professor Tiger does not expect to see the four "traditional" levels of biblical allegory—literal, allegorical, tropological, anagogical—at work in all instances of modern fabulation. My book will often discuss five simultaneous levels of meaning in Golding's novels: literal, moral, psychological, archetypal, and sociological.

13. Arnold Johnston, *Of Earth and Darkness: The Novels of William Golding*, p. 6.

14. See Northrop Frye, *Anatomy of Criticism: Four Essays*, pp. 90–91.

15. Edwin Honig, *Dark Conceit: The Making of Allegory*, p. 118. Honig mentions a fifth technique, "the allegorical waver," which concerns obvious correspondences evolving from within the story itself (coincidence, foreshadowing). Subsequent references are to this edition, and hereafter page numbers will be indicated in the text.

16. Kurt Weinberg, *Kafkas Dichtungen: Die Travestien des Mythos* (Bern-Munich: Franke, 1963), p. 238 (cited in Franz Kafka, *The Metamorphosis*, ed. Stanley Corngold, p. 64).

17. Norman Holland, "Realism and Unrealism: Kafka's 'Metamorphosis,'" *Modern Fiction Studies* 4 (Summer 1958): 149 (cited in Corngold edition of *The Metamorphosis*, p. 92).

18. Weinberg, *Dichtungen*, pp. 257–58 (cited in Corngold, p. 63).

19. James R. Baker, *William Golding: A Critical Study*, p. 44.

20. Fletcher, *Allegory*, p. 151.
21. Ibid., p. 154.
22. Edmund Reiss, *Elements of Literary Analysis*, p. 109.
23. C. S. Lewis, *The Allegory of Love*, p. 68.
24. Ibid., pp. 68–69.
25. Fletcher, *Allegory*, pp. 157–58.
26. Laurence Perrine, *Sound and Sense: An Introduction to Poetry*, p. 54.
27. René Wellek and Austin Warren, *Theory of Literature*, p. 178.
28. For additional modern studies that continue to classify allegory as an inferior form, see Erwin Panofsky, *Studies in Iconology*, p. 14. The author states that allegories deal with "conventional" subject matter, and use iconographical analysis "in the narrower sense of the word," while symbols involve "intrinsic meaning" and require interpretation "in a deeper sense." Also see Martin Foss, *Symbol and Metaphor in Human Experience*, p. 54, where the author says that "the length and copiousness of the details" in allegory make it an inadequate form.
29. Also see John J. White, *Mythology in the Modern Novel*, and Frank Kermode, "The Myth-Kitty," in *Puzzles and Epiphanies: Essays and Reviews, 1958–1961*, pp. 35–39.
30. See, respectively, Rubin Rabinovitz, *The Reaction Against Experiment in the English Novel, 1950–1960*, p. 36; Louis MacNeice, *Varieties of Parable*, pp. 146ff.; Scholes, *Fabulators*, p. 13.
31. Kingsley Amis, "*Pincher Martin*."
32. Angus Wilson, "Mood of the Month III," *London Magazine* 5 (April 1958): 44 (cited in Rabinovitz, *Reaction*, p. 65).

Chapter Two—Lord of the Flies

1. See Douglas Hewitt, "New Novels"; Francis E. Kearns, "Salinger and Golding: Conflict on the Campus," p. 139; Howard S. Babb, *The Novels of William Golding*, p. 19.
2. Margaret Walters, "Two Fabulists: Golding and Camus," p. 23. Walters criticizes *Lord of the Flies* for its "deliberate mystifications" paradoxically combined with "crude explicitness."
3. Walter Allen, "New Novels."
4. Clive Pemberton, *William Golding*, p. 9. For a detailed study of the close relationship between fantasy and realism in the modern novel, see Patrick Merla, "'What Is Real?' Asked the Rabbit One Day." A similar view is expressed by James Stern, "English Schoolboys in

the Jungle": "Fully to succeed, a fantasy must approach very close to reality."

5. Phillip Drew, "Second Reading," 79.
6. William Golding, *Lord of the Flies*, p. 65. Subsequent references are to this edition, and hereafter page numbers will be indicated in the text.
7. Wayland Young, "Letter from London," pp. 478–79.
8. Golding and Kermode, "Meaning," p. 10.
9. Baker, *Golding*, p. 9.
10. Bernard F. Dick, *William Golding*, p. 31.
11. William Mueller, "An Old Story Well Told: Commentary on William Golding's *Lord of the Flies*," p. 1203.
12. James Gindin, *Postwar British Fiction*, p. 198.
13. Ibid., p. 204. For other adverse criticism of Golding's "gimmick endings," see Young, "Letter," p. 481, and Kenneth Rexroth, "William Golding."
14. Dick, *Golding*, p. 21.
15. Baker, *Golding*, p. 10.
16. Bernard S. Oldsey and Stanley Weintraub, *The Art of William Golding*, p. 30.
17. Mark Kinkead-Weekes and Ian Gregor, *William Golding: A Critical Study*, p. 25.
18. Also see Robert J. White, "Butterfly and Beast in *Lord of the Flies*," in which he identifies the butterflies with the Greek word for butterfly, *psyche*, meaning "soul."
19. Oldsey and Weintraub, *Art*, p. 22.
20. Baker, *Golding*, p. 7. Also see Dick, *Golding*, pp. 29–33: "*Lord of the Flies* can also be read in the light of the Dionysian-Apollonian dichotomy" (i.e., the conflict between the irrational and rational worlds).
21. Granville Hicks, "The Evil that Lurks in the Heart," p. 36.
22. Golding, *Hot Gates*, pp. 86–87.
23. Keating and Golding, "Purdue Interview," pp. 189–90. Also see Douglas M. Davis, "A Conversation with Golding," p. 28; Maurice Dolbier, "Running J. D. Salinger a Close Second," p. 6.
24. Mueller, "Old Story," p. 1206.

Chapter Three—The Inheritors

1. Biles, *Talk*, p. 109. In this conversation entitled "Evil and Intelligence" (pp. 109–12), Golding distinguishes between "knowledge"

and "intelligence" and agrees with Biles's statement that "guilt and intelligence equate, instead of guilt and knowledge."

2. Dick, *Golding*, p. 39; Baker, *Golding*, p. 23; Samuel Hynes, *William Golding*, p. 16; Paul Elmen, *William Golding*, p. 25.

3. See George Plimpton, "Without the Evil to Endure," p. 21; William James Smith, "A Hopeless Struggle against Homo Sapiens"; Diana Neill, *A Short History of the English Novel*, p. 387; Frederick R. Karl, *A Reader's Guide to the Contemporary English Novel*, p. 259; Rexroth, "Golding," p. 98; Frank MacShane, "The Novels of William Golding," p. 174.

4. See particularly Book II, "The Making of Man," in H. G. Wells, *The Outline of History*, pp. 50–104.

5. Ibid., pp. 69–70.

6. Ibid., p. 69.

7. Golding and Kermode, "Meaning", p. 10.

8. Ibid.

9. Dolbier, "Running," p. 6.

10. See Peter Green, "The World of William Golding," pp. 45–46.

11. See Biles, *Talk*, p. 107.

12. See Brian W. Aldiss, *Billion Year Spree: The True History of Science Fiction*, p. 117; and Oldsey and Weintraub, *Art*, p. 53. There are only coincidental similarities between Golding's novel and Vardis Fisher's *The Golden Rooms*, contrary to Kirby Duncan, "William Golding and Vardis Fisher: A Study in Parallels and Extensions." In correspondence, Golding told me that he had never heard of the Fisher novel.

13. Hynes, *Golding*, p. 18.

14. Babb, *Novels*, p. 40.

15. William Golding, *The Inheritors* p. 35. Subsequent references are to this edition, and hereafter page numbers will be indicated in the text.

16. Walter Sullivan, "The Long Chronicle of Guilt: William Golding's *The Spire*," p. 3.

17. Baker, *Golding*, p. 29.

18. Ibid., p. 30.

19. Leighton Hodson, *William Golding*, pp. 49–50.

20. W. W. Robson, *Modern English Literature*, p. 156.

21. Albert Cook, *Prisms: Studies in Modern Literature*, pp. 122–23.

1. Oldsey and Weintraub, *Art*, p. 76.
2. Rexroth, "Golding," p. 97.
3. Golding to Biles, *Talk*, p. 77.
4. I use one of Golding's favorite expressions when he is describing his ironic versions of established ideas or literary precedents. See, e.g., Biles, *Talk*, pp. 4 and 99.
5. Oldsey and Weintraub, *Art*, p. 92.
6. Quoted in Kermode, *Puzzles*, pp. 207–8.
7. William Golding, *Pincher Martin*, p. 8. There is no American cloth-bound edition of this book in print. Subsequent references are to this edition, and hereafter page numbers will be indicated in the text.
8. Kermode, *Puzzles*, p. 208.
9. Charles M. Gayley, *The Classic Myths in English Literature and in Art*, p. 11.
10. See Oldsey and Weintraub, *Art*, p. 95; John Bowen, "Bending Over Backwards"; Walters, "Fabulists," p. 25.
11. Norman Podhoretz, "The Two Deaths of Christopher Martin," p. 189.
12. Golding and Kermode, "Meaning," p. 10.
13. Weekes and Gregor, *Golding*, p. 128.
14. Dick, *Golding*, p. 57.
15. John Peter, "The Fables of William Golding," p. 588.
16. Cf. Nathaniel Hawthorne, "Egotism; or, The Bosom Serpent," *The Complete Novels and Selected Tales*, pp. 1107–16: "Strange specta-cle in human life where it is the instinctive effort of one and all to hide those sad realities, and leave them undisturbed beneath a heap of superficial topics" (p. 1112).
17. Elmen, *Golding*, pp. 29–30.
18. Quoted by Owen Webster, "Free Fall," *John O'London's Weekly* (January 28, 1960), p. 90 [repr. in *A Library of Literary Criticism: Modern British Literature*, ed. Ruth Z. Temple and Martin Tucker, 1:353].
19. MacNeice, *Varieties*, p. 148.
20. Regarding the connection between Golding's own poetry and the imagery of *Pincher Martin*, see Cecil W. Davies, "The Novels Fore-shadowed: Some Recurring Themes in Early Poems by William Golding," p. 88. Also see MacShane, "Novels," p. 181: "He [Golding] is, in short, a poet."

21. Irving Malin, "The Elements of William Golding," pp. 43–44.
22. Hodson, *Golding*, p. 65.
23. John Peter, "Postscript," p. 34. Also see Jeanne Delbaere-Garant, "From the Cellar to the Rock: A Recurrent Pattern in William Golding's Novels."
24. Ralph Freedman, "The New Realism: The Fancy of William Golding," p. 126.
25. Oldsey and Weintraub, *Art*, pp. 98–99.
26. Freedman, "Realism," p. 126.
27. See particularly *"Pincher Martin* and Free Will," in Biles, *Talk*, pp. 73–77.
28. James Gindin, "The Fable Begins to Break Down," pp. 3–4.
29. See Golding and Kermode, "Meaning," p. 10: "If you are not a Christian and die, . . . your purgatory, or your heaven or your hell won't have the Christian attributes."
30. Dick, *Golding*, p. 99.

Chapter Five—Free Fall

1. H. McKeating, "The Significance of William Golding," p. 331; Baker, *Golding*, p. 62; Bernard F. Dick, *"The Pyramid*: Mr. Golding's 'New' Novel," p. 86; Hynes, *Golding*, p. 33; Pemberton, *Golding*, pp. 19–20.
2. Weekes and Gregor, *Golding*, p. 165. These two critics, while emphasizing the theme of becoming, recognize that *Free Fall* explores both modes, being and becoming, simultaneously.
3. In contrast to Weekes and Gregor, Howard Babb, *Novels*, p. 100, believes that *Free Fall* is more concerned with states of being than becoming: "this novel seems in some ways static: aimed at defining the condition of a man rather than moving toward some clear-cut narrative and thematic resolution of his state."
4. Ibid., p. 97; also see Pemberton, *Golding*, p. 10.
5. Michael P. Gallagher, "The Human Image in William Golding," pp. 203–4.
6. Ibid., p. 205.
7. Baker, *Golding*, p. 58.
8. See Owen Webster, "Living with Chaos," p. 15.
9. William Golding, *Free Fall*, p. 5. There is no American clothbound edition of this novel in print. Subsequent references are to this edition, and hereafter page numbers will be indicated in the text.
10. Baker, *Golding*, p. 65.

11. See Hodson, *Golding*, p. 87; and Weekes and Gregor, *Golding*, p. 186.
12. Oldsey and Weintraub, *Art*, p. 111.
13. Weekes and Gregor, *Golding*, p. 177.
14. Oldsey and Weintraub, *Art*, p. 113.
15. In Biles, *Talk*, pp. 81–82, Golding states that one of the underlying myths of *Free Fall* is "the Genesis idea."
16. Frank Kermode, "The Novels of William Golding," p. 26.
17. Baker, *Golding*, p. 61; also see Hodson, *Golding*, pp. 75 and 83.
18. See Michael D. Feinstein, "The Innocent, the Wicked, and the Guilty in the Novels of William Golding."
19. Babb, *Novels*, p. 127.
20. Delbaere-Garant, "Cellar," p. 511.
21. Baker, *Golding*, p. 65.
22. Biles, *Talk*, p. 81.
23. For a discussion of the theme of regeneration and deliverance in *Free Fall*, see Kermode, "The Novels of William Golding," p. 28; Peter M. Axthelm, *The Modern Confessional Novel*, pp. 126–27; and Weekes and Gregor, *Golding*, pp. 196–99, who eventually, however, arrive at a wholly self-defeating critical view: "The moment we fail Golding's challenge and 'reduce' the cryptograms, we too are on the slippery slope. It is only in riddle, in dense opacity, total ambiguity that things can be seen as they really are."

Chapter Six—The Spire

1. Baker, *Golding*, p. 79.
2. William Golding, *The Spire*, p. 76. Subsequent references are to this edition, and hereafter page numbers will be indicated in the text.
3. Several critics have noted the parallels to Ibsen: see Dick, *Golding*, p. 100; Thomas P. McDonnell, "System-Building," p. 378; Gallagher, "Image," p. 209; and especially Oldsey and Weintraub, *Art*, pp. 133–40.
4. Biles, *Talk*, p. 100.
5. Ibid., p. 98.
6. Hynes, *Golding*, p. 45.
7. Arthur R. Hogue, "Jocelin of Brakelond."
8. Donald Nicholl, "Jocelin of Wells."
9. In addition, Golding has stated that he wanted the name to be something more than merely "medieval-sounding," so he selected the name of one of his contemporary acquaintances, thus combin-

ing both past and present in one name. See Biles, *Talk*, p. 98: "It was not only medieval; there are still people called Jocelin. I know at least one person called Jocelin. I wanted something which would fit."

10. William Barrett, "Reader's Choice," p. 135.
11. Gallagher, "Image," p. 210.
12. Babb, *Novels*, p. 152.
13. Weekes and Gregor, *Golding*, p. 211.
14. Hodson, *Golding*, p. 97.
15. Babb, *Novels*, p. 151.
16. Frank Kermode, *Continuities*, p. 192.
17. David Skilton, "Golding's *The Spire*," p. 55.
18. Delbaere-Garant, "Cellar," p. 510.
19. Skilton, "Golding's," p. 49.
20. Delbaere-Garant, "Cellar," p. 512.
21. Hodson, *Golding*, p. 96.
22. Weekes and Gregor, *Golding*, p. 235.
23. Ibid.
24. McDonnell, "System-Building," pp. 377–78.
25. Paul Pickrel, "The Cost of Vision," p. 120.
26. Weekes and Gregor, *Golding*, pp. 223–24.
27. Dick, *Golding*, p. 87.

Chapter Seven—The Pyramid

1. Hynes, *Golding*, pp. 45–46; Granville Hicks, "Caste in a Comedy of Manners"; Doris Grumbach, "The Pyramid"; Robert J. Clements, "European Literary Scene"; William B. Hill, "*The Pyramid*"; Roderick Cook, "Books in Brief," p. 130; Rachel Trickett, "Recent Novels: Craftsmanship in Violence and Sex."
2. Frederick R. Karl, *A Reader's Guide to the Contemporary English Novel*, rev. ed., p. 333. Karl sometimes misreads Golding: in his "re-evaluation" of *Lord of the Flies*, p. 334, he entirely misses the irony in the naval officer's appearance.
3. John Wakeman, "Three in One: *The Pyramid*," p. 4.
4. Arnold Johnston, "Innovation and Rediscovery in Golding's *The Pyramid*," p. 106.
5. Marshall Walker, "William Golding: From Paradigm to Pyramid," p. 80.
6. Wakeman, "Three in One," p. 5.
7. Karl, *A Reader's Guide*, rev. ed., p. 333. Johnston, "Innovation," pp.

106–10, in an ingenious but not totally convincing discussion, sees *The Pyramid* as an ironic treatment of Dickens's *Great Expectations*. David Skilton, "*The Pyramid* and Comic Social Fiction," in *William Golding: Some Critical Considerations*, ed. Biles and Evans, pp. 184–85, traces parallels with Trollope's *The Last Chronicle of Barset*.

8. Golding, *Hot Gates*, p. 127.
9. Ibid., p. 128. Oldsey and Weintraub, *Art*, p. 163, quote at length the Wells passage from *Mr. Polly*, and conclude that it "is possible to view almost the entire Golding oeuvre as an implicit response to this Wellsian image."
10. Golding, *Hot Gates*, p. 128.
11. Ibid., p. 130.
12. Ibid., p. 168.
13. Golding, *Free Fall*, p. 193.
14. Golding, *Hot Gates*, p. 81.
15. Dick, "*Pyramid*," p. 86.
16. See Grumbach, "Pyramid," p. 721.
17. William Golding, *The Pyramid*, p. 8. Subsequent references are to this edition, and hereafter page numbers will be indicated in the text.
18. Pemberton, *Golding*, p. 25.
19. This conversation occurs prior to the meeting with Evie, but it is narrated in the second section of the novel.
20. The motif of freedom versus confinement is a unifying secondary theme; see *The Pyramid*, pp. 70, 122, and 151.
21. Golding, *Hot Gates*, p. 74.
22. Johnston, "Innovation," p. 102; also see Dick, "*Pyramid*," pp. 93–94. For further discussion of how music metaphors affect the novel, see Stephen Medcalf, *William Golding*, pp. 37–39.

Chapter Eight—The Later Novels

1. Bernard Oldsey, "Salinger and Golding: Resurrection or Repose," pp. 136, 138. Oldsey plays devil's advocate, for he would have surely been aware of the forthcoming publication of *Darkness Visible*, especially since Golding's change of publisher and resultant legal problems received considerable coverage in the American press.
2. Brad Owens, "Golding's New Morality Tale: Hard to Believe," p. 24. For other negative reviews, see Paul Ableman, "Ignorable Ruin";

Thomas LeClair, "Golding's 'Darkness'" Is Mainly a Sermon."

3. John Calvin Batchelor, "Golding Beats the Devil," p. 43. For other, more modestly favorable reactions, see Benjamin DeMott, "Short Reviews"; Peter S. Prescott, "The Inferno—Here and Now"; Craig Raine, "Between the Stars."

4. Joyce Carol Oates, "Darkness Visible," p. 32.

5. C. Day Lewis, *The Aeneid of Virgil*, p. 137.

6. Oates, "Darkness," p. 32; DeMott, "Review," p. 92; Doris Grumbach, "Parables of Darkness"; Batchelor, "Golding," p. 47; Owens, "Golding's," p. 24; Frank Tuohy, "Baptism by Fire."

7. John Thompson, "Magic Fable," p. 55.

8. Tiger, *Golding*, p. 228.

9. William Golding, *Darkness Visible*, p. 16. Subsequent references are to this edition, and hereafter page numbers will be indicated in the text.

10. For a detailed analysis of biblical analogues in *Darkness Visible*, see Don Crompton, *A View from the Spire: William Golding's Later Novels*, pp. 94–126. However, Crompton does not seem to recognize the allusion to Ezekiel's wheels.

11. Ibid., pp. 102–3, believes that Matty merely flings his shoe as he utters the biblical curse and that Henderson then falls on the exact spot where the shoe lands. Arnold Johnstone, *Of Earth and Darkness*, p. 101, simply calls Henderson's death a suicide, never refers to Matty's biblical allusion, and maintains that Matty is completely "innocent."

12. Little critical reaction has focused on the humor of *Darkness Visible*. For a view that recognizes some of this comic tone, see Nigel Dennis, "Smiles in the Dark."

13. Bernard F. Dick, "'The Novelist Is a Displaced Person': An Interview with William Golding," p. 482. For a view of the "terrifying and inexplicable Oneness" of the polarized forces represented by Sophy and Matty, see Cecil Davies, "'The Burning Bird': Golding's Poems and the Novels," pp. 114–15.

14. Derwent May, "Fiery Fanaticism," p. 49.

15. Crompton, *View*, p. 157.

16. Jean Strouse, "All at Sea."

17. Nereo E. Condini, "*Rites of Passage*."

18. George Stade, "Sailing Through Symbolic Seas," p. 38.

19. Robert Towers, "The Good Ship Britannia," p. 8.

20. James R. Baker, "An Interview with William Golding," p. 164.
21. William Golding, *Rites of Passage*, p. 275. Subsequent references are to this edition, and hereafter page numbers will be indicated in the text.
22. Herbert Mitgang, "William Golding's World."
23. Baker, "Interview," p. 162.
24. Ibid.
25. Ibid., p. 161. Also see John Haffenden, *Novelists in Interview*, p. 100.
26. Ibid., p. 132.
27. Kay Larson, "Book Briefs."
28. Grove Koger, "*Rites of Passage*."
29. Vincent D. Balitas, "*Rites of Passage*," p. 40.
30. Baker, "Interview," p. 132. For a more elaborate discussion of theatrical elements in *Rites*, see Crompton, *View*, pp. 131–33.
31. William Golding, *The Paper Men*, p. 106. Subsequent references are to this edition, and hereafter page numbers will be indicated in the text.
32. William Golding, *A Moving Target*, pp. 9–19.
33. Tiger, *Golding*, p. 13.
34. Golding, *Hot Gates*, pp. 140–56.
35. Biles, *Talk*, pp. ix–x.
36. Golding, *Target*, p. 169.
37. Ibid.
38. Jonathan Raban, "Novelist as Preacher," p. 144.
39. Paul Gray, "Mutters of Life and Death."
40. Golding, *Target*, p. 170.

Chapter Nine—Appraisals of a Writer in Progress

1. Babb, *Novels*, p. 203.
2. Dick, "*Pyramid*," p. 89.
3. Biles, *Talk*, p. 7.
4. William Golding, *The Scorpion God*, pp. 63–114.
5. Biles, *Talk*, p. 66.

Bibliography

Ableman, Paul. "Ignorable Ruin." *Spectator* 243 (October 1979): 23.

Aldiss, Brian W. *Billion Year Spree: The True History of Science Fiction.* Garden City, NY: Doubleday and Company, 1973.

Allen, Walter. "New Novels." *New Statesman* 48 (September 25, 1954): 370.

Amis, Kingsley. "*Pincher Martin.*" *Spectator* 197 (November 9, 1956): 656.

Axthelm, Peter M. *The Modern Confessional Novel.* New Haven: Yale University Press, 1967.

Babb, Howard S. *The Novels of William Golding.* Columbus: Ohio State University Press, 1970.

Baker, James R. "An Interview with William Golding." *Twentieth Century Literature* 28 (Summer 1982): 130–70.

———. *William Golding: A Critical Study.* New York: St. Martin's Press, 1965.

Baker, James R., and Arthur P. Ziegler, Jr., eds. *Lord of the Flies: Text, Notes and Criticism.* New York: G. P. Putnam's Sons, 1964.

Balitas, Vincent D. "*Rites of Passage.*" *America* 145 (July 25, 1981): 39–40.

Barrett, William. "Reader's Choice." *Atlantic Monthly* 213 (May 1964): 135–36.

Batchelor, John Calvin. "Golding Beats the Devil." *The Village Voice* 24 (November 5, 1979): 43, 47.

Biles, Jack I. *Talk: Conversations with William Golding*. New York: Harcourt Brace Jovanovich, 1970.

Biles, Jack I., and Robert O. Evans, eds. *William Golding: Some Critical Considerations*. Lexington: University Press of Kentucky, 1978.

Bowen, John. "Bending Over Backwards." *Times Literary Supplement* 3008 (October 23, 1959): 608.

Clements, Robert J. "European Literary Scene." *Saturday Review* 50 (July 1, 1967): 19, 28.

Condini, Nereo E. *"Rites of Passage." National Review* 33 (October 30, 1981): 1289.

Cook, Albert. *Prisms: Studies in Modern Literature*. Bloomington: Indiana University Press, 1967.

Cook, Roderick. "Books in Brief." *Harper's Magazine* 235 (November 1967): 129–30.

Crompton, Don. *A View from the Spire: William Golding's Later Novels*. Oxford: Basil Blackwell, 1985.

Davies, Cecil W. "'The Burning Bird': Golding's Poems and the Novels." *Studies in the Literary Imagination* 13 (Spring 1980): 97–117.

———. "The Novels Foreshadowed: Some Recurring Themes in Early Poems by William Golding." *English* 17 (Autumn 1968): 86–89.

Davis, Douglas M. "A Conversation with Golding." *The New Republic* 148 (May 4, 1963): 28–30.

Delbaere-Garant, Jeanne. "From the Cellar to the Rock: A Recurrent Pattern in William Golding's Novels." *Modern Fiction Studies* 17 (Winter 1971–72): 501–12.

DeMott, Benjamin. "Short Reviews." *Atlantic Monthly* 244 (November 1979): 92.

Dennis, Nigel. "Smiles in the Dark." *New York Review of Books* 26 (December 6, 1979): 42.

Dick, Bernard F. "'The Novelist Is a Displaced Person': An Interview with William Golding." *College English* 26 (March 1965): 480–82.

———. *"The Pyramid*: Mr. Golding's 'New' Novel." *Studies in the Literary Imagination* 2 (October 1969): 83–95.

———. *William Golding*. New York: Twayne Publishers, 1967.

Dolbier, Maurice. "Running J. D. Salinger a Close Second." *New York Herald Tribune Books* 38 (May 20, 1962): 6, 15.

Drew, Philip. "Second Reading." *The Cambridge Review* 78 (October 27, 1956): 79, 81, 83–84.

Duncan, Kirby. "William Golding and Vardis Fisher: A Study in Parallels and Extensions." *College English* 27 (December 1965): 232–35.

Elmen, Paul. *William Golding*. Grand Rapids, MI: William B. Eerdmans, 1967.

Feinstein, Michael D. "The Innocent, the Wicked, and the Guilty in the Novels of William Golding." Master's thesis, Miami University, Oxford, OH, 1965.

Fletcher, Angus. *Allegory: The Theory of a Symbolic Mode*. Ithaca: Cornell University Press, 1964.

Foss, Martin. *Symbol and Metaphor in Human Experience*. Lincoln: University of Nebraska Press, 1949.

Freedman, Ralph. "The New Realism: The Fancy of William Golding." *Perspective* 10 (Summer–Autumn 1958): 118–28.

Frye, Northrop. *Anatomy of Criticism: Four Essays*. Princeton: Princeton University Press, 1957.

Gallagher, Michael P. "The Human Image in William Golding." *Studies* 54 (Summer–Autumn 1965): 197–216.

Gayley, Charles M. *The Classic Myths in English Literature and in Art*. Boston: Ginn and Company, 1911.

Gindin, James. "The Fable Begins to Break Down." *Wisconsin Studies in Contemporary Literature* 8 (Winter 1967): 1–18.

———. *Postwar British Fiction*. Berkeley: University of California Press, 1962.

Golding, William. *Darkness Visible*. New York: Farrar, Straus and Giroux, 1979.

———. *Free Fall*. 1959; repr. New York: Harcourt, Brace and World, 1962.

———. *The Hot Gates and Other Occasional Pieces*. New York: Harcourt, Brace and World, 1966.

———. *The Inheritors*. 1955; repr. New York: Harcourt, Brace and World, 1962.

———. *Lord of the Flies*. 1954; repr. New York: Coward, McCann and Geoghegan, 1962.

———. *A Moving Target*. New York: Farrar, Straus and Giroux, 1982.

———. *The Paper Men*. New York: Farrar, Straus and Giroux, 1984.

———. *Pincher Martin*. 1956; repr. New York: Harcourt, Brace and World, 1957.

———. *The Pyramid*. New York: Harcourt, Brace and World, 1967.

———. *Rites of Passage*. New York: Farrar, Straus and Giroux, 1980.

———. *The Scorpion God*. New York: Harcourt Brace Jovanovich, 1972.

————. *The Spire*. New York: Harcourt, Brace and World, 1964.

Golding, William, and Frank Kermode. "The Meaning of It All." *Books and Bookmen*, 5 (October 1959): 9–10.

Gray, Paul. "Mutters of Life and Death." *Time* 123 (April 9, 1984): 98.

Green, Peter. "The World of William Golding." *Transactions and Proceedings of the Royal Society of Literature* 32 (1963): 37–57.

Grumbach, Doris. "Parables of Darkness." *Books and Arts* (December 21, 1979), p. 9.

————. "*The Pyramid*." *America* 117 (December 9, 1967): 720–21.

Haffenden, John. *Novelists in Interview*. London: Methuen, 1985.

Hawthorne, Nathaniel. *The Complete Novels and Selected Tales*. Ed. Norman H. Pearson. New York: Modern Library, 1937.

Hewitt, Douglas. "New Novels." *The Manchester Guardian* 71 (September 28, 1954): 4.

Hicks, Granville. "Caste in a Comedy of Manners." *Saturday Review* 50 (October 14, 1967): 25–26.

————. "The Evil that Lurks in the Heart." *Saturday Review* 47 (April 18, 1964): 35–36.

Hill, William B. "*The Pyramid*." *America* 117 (November 25, 1967): 666.

Hodson, Leighton. *William Golding*. Edinburgh: Oliver and Boyd, 1969.

Hogue, Arthur R. "Jocelin of Brakelond." *New Catholic Encyclopedia* New York: McGraw-Hill, 1967.

Holman, C. Hugh, W. F. Thrall, and Addison Hibbard. *A Handbook to Literature*. 3d ed. Indianapolis: Bobbs-Merrill, 1972.

Honig, Edwin. *Dark Conceit: The Making of Allegory*. Evanston: Northwestern University Press, 1959.

Hynes, Samuel. *William Golding*. 2d ed. New York: Columbia University Press, 1968.

Johnston, Arnold. "Innovation and Rediscovery in Golding's *The Pyramid*." *Critique: Studies in Modern Fiction* 14 (1972): 97–112.

————. *Of Earth and Darkness: The Novels of William Golding*. Columbia: University of Missouri Press, 1980.

Kafka, Franz. *The Metamorphosis*. Ed. Stanley Corngold. New York: Bantam Books, 1972.

Karl, Frederick R. *A Reader's Guide to the Contemporary English Novel*. New York: Farrar, Straus and Company, 1962.

————. *A Reader's Guide to the Contemporary English Novel*. Rev. ed. New York: Farrar, Straus and Giroux, 1972.

Kearns, Francis E. "Salinger and Golding: Conflict on the Campus." *America* 108 (January 26, 1963): 136–39.

Keating, James, and William Golding. "Purdue Interview." In *Lord of the Flies: Text, Notes and Criticism*, ed. James R. Baker and Arthur P. Ziegler, Jr., q.v.

Kellogg, Robert, and Oliver Steele, eds. *Books I and II of "The Faerie Queene."* New York: Odyssey Press, 1965.

Kermode, Frank. *Continuities*. New York: Random House, 1968.

————. "The Novels of William Golding." *International Literary Annual* 3 (1961): 11–29.

————. *Puzzles and Epiphanies: Essays and Reviews, 1958–1961*. New York: Chilmark Press, 1962.

Kinkead-Weekes, Mark, and Ian Gregor. *William Golding: A Critical Study*. New York: Harcourt, Brace and World, 1968.

Koger, Grove. *"Rites of Passage." Library Journal* 105 (October 1, 1980): 2106.

Larson, Kay. "Book Briefs." *Saturday Review* 7 (October 1980): 86.

LeClair, Thomas. "Golding's 'Darkness' Is Mainly a Sermon." *Cincinnati Enquirer*, December 23, 1979, p. E9.

Lewis, C. Day. *The Aeneid of Virgil*. Garden City, NY: Doubleday Anchor, 1952.

Lewis, C. S. *The Allegory of Love*. 1936; repr. New York: Oxford University Press, 1958.

McDonnell, Thomas P. "System-Building." *Commonweal* 80 (June 12, 1964): 377–79.

McKeating, H. "The Significance of William Golding." *The Expository Times* 79 (August 1968): 329–33.

MacNeice, Louis. *Varieties of Parable*. Cambridge: Cambridge University Press, 1965.

MacQueen, John. *Allegory*. London: Methuen and Company, 1970.

MacShane, Frank. "The Novels of William Golding." *Dalhousie Review* 42 (Summer 1962): 171–83.

Malin, Irving, "The Elements of William Golding." In *Contemporary British Novelists*, ed. Charles Shapiro, q.v.

May, Derwent. "Fiery Fanaticism." *Saturday Review* 7 (January 5, 1980): 48–49.

Medcalf, Stephen. *William Golding*. London: Longman, 1975.

Merla, Patrick. "'What Is Real?' Asked the Rabbit One Day." *Saturday Review* 55 (November 4, 1972): 43–50.

Mitgang, Herbert. "William Golding's World." *New York Times Book Review*, November 2, 1980, p. 47.

Mueller, William. "An Old Story Well Told: Commentary on William

Golding's *Lord of the Flies.*" *Christian Century* 80 (October 2, 1963): 1203–6.

Neill, Diana. *A Short History of the English Novel.* Rev. ed. New York: Collier Books, 1964.

Nelson, William, ed. *Lord of the Flies: A Source Book.* New York: Odyssey Press, 1963.

Nicholl, Donald. "Jocelin of Wells." *New Catholic Encyclopedia.* New York: McGraw-Hill, 1967.

Niemann, Thomas C. "'Pearl' and the Medieval Christian Doctrine of Salvation." Ph.D. dissertation, Duke University, Durham, NC, 1971.

Oates, Joyce Carol. "*Darkness Visible.*" *The New Republic* 181 (December 8, 1979): 32–34.

Oldsey, Bernard. "Salinger and Golding: Resurrection or Repose." *College Literature* 6 (Spring 1979): 136–44.

Oldsey, Bernard S., and Stanley Weintraub. *The Art of William Golding.* 1965; repr. Bloomington: Indiana University Press, 1968.

Owens, Brad. "Golding's New Morality Tale: Hard to Believe." *Christian Science Monitor,* November 28, 1979, p. 24.

Panofsky, Erwin. *Studies in Iconology: Humanistic Themes in the Art of the Renaissance.* 1939; repr. New York: Harper and Row, 1962.

Pemberton, Clive. *William Golding.* London: Longmans, Green and Company, 1969.

Perrine, Lawrence. *Sound and Sense: An Introduction to Poetry.* 3d ed. New York: Harcourt, Brace and World, 1969.

Peter, John. "The Fables of Willaim Golding." *Kenyon Review* 19 (Autumn 1957): 577–92.

―――. "Postscript." In *Lord of the Flies: A Source Book,* ed. Willian Nelson, q.v.

Pickrel, Paul. "The Cost of Vision." *Harper's Magazine* 228 (May 1964): 119–20.

Piehler, Paul. *The Visionary Landscape: A Study in Medieval Allegory.* Montreal: McGill-Queen's University Press, 1971.

Plimpton, George. "Without the Evil to Endure." *New York Times Book Review,* July 29, 1962, pp. 4, 21.

Podhoretz, Norman, "*The Two Deaths of Christopher Martin.*" *New Yorker* 33 (September 21, 1957): 189–90.

Prescott, Peter S. "The Inferno—Here and Now." *Newsweek* 94 (November 5, 1979): 108.

Raban, Jonathan. "Novelist as Preacher." *Atlantic Monthly* 253 (April 1984): 142, 144–45.

Rabinovitz, Rubin. *The Reaction Against Experiment in the English Novel, 1950–1960*. New York: Columbia University Press, 1967.

Raine, Craig. "Between the Stars." *New Statesman* 98 (October 12, 1979): 552–53.

Reiss, Edmund. *Elements of Literary Analysis*. Cleveland: World Publishing Company, 1967.

Rexroth, Kenneth. "William Golding." *Atlantic Monthly* 215 (May 1965): 96–98.

Robson, W. W. *Modern English Literature*. London: Oxford University Press, 1970.

Scholes, Robert. *The Fabulators*. New York: Oxford University Press, 1967.

Shapiro, Charles, ed. *Contemporary British Novelists*. Carbondale: Southern Illinois University Press, 1965.

Skilton, David. "Golding's *The Spire*." *Studies in the Literary Imagination* 2 (October 1969): 45–56.

———. "*The Pyramid* and Comic Social Fiction." In *William Golding: Some Critical Considerations*, ed. Jack I. Biles and Robert O. Evans, q.v.

Smith, William James. "A Hopeless Struggle against Homo Sapiens." *Commonweal* 77 (September 28, 1962): 19.

Stade, George. "Sailing Through Symbolic Seas." *New York Times Book Review*, November 2, 1980, pp. 7, 38–39.

Stern, James. "English Schoolboys in the Jungle." *New York Times Book Review*, October 23, 1955, p. 38.

Strouse, Jean. "All at Sea." *Newsweek* 96 (October 27, 1980): 104.

Sullivan, Walter. "The Long Chronicle of Guilt: William Golding's *The Spire*." *The Hollins Critic* 1 (June 1964): 1–12.

Temple, Ruth Z., and Martin Tucker, eds. *A Library of Literary Criticism: Modern British Literature*. 3 vols. New York: Frederick Ungar, 1966.

Thompson, John. "Magic Fable." *New York Times Book Review*, November 18, 1979, pp. 1, 54–55.

Tiger, Virginia. *William Golding: The Dark Fields of Discovery*. London: Calder & Boyars, 1974.

Towers, Robert. "The Good Ship Britannia." *New York Review of Books* 27 (December 18, 1980): 4, 6, 8.

Trickett, Rachel. "Recent Novels: Craftsmanship in Violence and Sex." *Yale Review* 57 (March 1968): 438–52.

Tuohy, Frank. "Baptism by Fire." *Times Literary Supplement* 4001 (November 23, 1979): 41.

Wakeman, John. "Three in One: *The Pyramid.*" *New York Times Book Review*, October 15, 1967, pp. 4–5, 42.

Walker, Marshall. "William Golding: From Paradigm to Pyramid." *Studies in the Literary Imagination* 2 (October 1969): 67–82.

Walters, Margaret. "Two Fabulists: Golding and Camus." *Melbourne Critical Review* 4 (1961): 18–29.

Webster, Owen. "Living with Chaos." *Books and Art*, March 1958, pp. 15–16.

Wellek, René, and Austin Warren. *Theory of Literature.* 2d ed. New York: Harcourt, Brace and Company, 1956.

Wells, H. G. *The Outline of History.* Rev. ed. Garden City, NY: Garden City Books, 1961.

White, John J. *Mythology in the Modern Novel: A Study of Prefigurative Techniques.* Princeton: Princeton University Press, 1971.

White, Robert J. "Butterfly and Beast in *Lord of the Flies.*" *Modern Fiction Studies* 10 (Summer 1964): 163–70.

Young, Wayland. "Letter from London." *Kenyon Review* 19 (Summer 1957): 478–82.

Index

Names of characters in Golding's novels are followed by the title of the book in which they appear.

Abraham and Isaac, 81–82
Action compared to a state of mind: defined, 7; in *Darkness Visible*, 114; in *Free Fall*, 63–65; in *The Inheritors*, 32; in *Lord of the Flies*, 16; in *Pincher Martin*, 47–49; in *The Pyramid*, 101–3; in *Rites of Passage*, 122; in *The Spire*, 82–83
Adam, 63, 73, 94, 101
Adam, Father (*The Spire*), 79, 82, 89, 92–93
Agave, 15–16
Ajax, 45, 47
Alfred (*Pincher Martin*), 47–48
Alison, Lady (*The Spire*), 85, 87, 89
Allegory: compared to symbolism, 3; defined, 1–2, 11; Golding on, 3; Greek and Roman narrative, 2; as inferior literary form, 141n28; medieval, and its double force, 4–5, 140n10; and the modern novel, 1–11; and myth, 11; naive, 2, 4, 59; and narrative, 139n8
Allen, Walter, 12
Alsopp, Robert (*Free Fall*), 64, 68
Amis, Kingsley, 11

Anderson, Captain (*Rites of Passage*), 120, 126
Anselm (*Free Fall*), 64
Anselm (*The Spire*), 85, 87–89
Aristotle, 120
Arnold, Philip (*Free Fall*), 64–65, 67–68

Babb, Howard, 81
Baker, James, 15, 24, 34–35, 119
Balitas, Vincent, 124
Ballantyne, R. M., 17, 42, 77; *The Coral Island*, 13–14, 28, 99
Barclay, Wilfred (*The Paper Men*), 127–33
Batchelor, John, 110
Battle motif: defined, 8–9; in *Darkness Visible*, 114–15; in *Free Fall*, 67–70; in *The Inheritors*, 33–36; in *Lord of the Flies*, 18–19; in *Pincher Martin*, 51–53; in *The Pyramid*, 104–6; in *Rites of Passage*, 123–24; in *The Spire*, 85–89
Beatrice (*Free Fall*), 61–62, 64–69, 71–72, 83, 137
Beelzebub, 19, 21
Being and Becoming, 58–59
Bell, Edwin (*Darkness Visible*), 115
Bell, Edwina (*Darkness Visible*), 115
Bierce, Ambrose, 43; "An Occurrence at Owl Creek Bridge, " 42
Biles, Jack, 129

159

DATE DUE

~~DEC 1 5~~	
~~APR 1 1 1996~~	~~DEC 0 8 1998~~
~~DEC 1 3 1996~~	
~~MAR 0 1996~~	~~OCT 9 0 1996~~
~~FEB 2 0 19~~	~~MAY 2 2 2008~~
~~APR 3 0 1996~~	
~~NOV 0 8 1998~~	
~~FEB 1 9 2008~~	